The Poetry of Laurence Binyon

Volume III - Porphyrion & Other Poems

Robert Laurence Binyon, CH, was born on August 10th, 1869 in Lancaster in Lancashire, England to Quaker parents, Frederick Binyon and Mary Dockray.

He studied at St Paul's School, London before enrolling at Trinity College, Oxford, to read classics.

Binyon's first published work was Persephone in 1890. As a poet, his output was not prodigious and, in the main, the volumes he did publish were slim. But his reputation was of the highest order. When the Poet Laureate, Alfred Austin, died in 1913, Binyon was considered alongside Thomas Hardy and Rudyard Kipling for the post which was given to Robert Bridges.

Binyon played a pivotal role in helping to establish the modernist School of poetry and introduced imagist poets such as Ezra Pound, Richard Aldington and H.D. (Hilda Doolittle) to East Asian visual art and literature. Most of his career was spent at The British Museum where he produced many books particularly centering on the art of the Far East.

Moved and shaken by the onset of the World War I and its military tactics of young men slaughtered to hold or gain a few yards of shell-shocked mud Binyon wrote his seminal poem For the Fallen. It became an instant classic, turning moments of great loss into a National and human tribute.

After the war, he returned to the British Museum and wrote numerous books on art; especially on William Blake, Persian and Japanese art.

In 1931, his two volume Collected Poems appeared and in 1933, he retired from the British Museum.

Between 1933 and 1943, Binyon published his acclaimed translation of Dante's Divine Comedy in an English version of terza rima.

During the Second World War Binyon wrote another poetic masterpiece 'The Burning of the Leaves', about the London Blitz.

Robert Laurence Binyon died in Dunedin Nursing Home, Bath Road, Reading, on March 10th, 1943 after undergoing an operation.

Index of Contents

PORPHYRION

A POEM, IN FIVE BOOKS

ARGUMENT

A young man of Antioch, flying from the world, in that enthusiasm for the ascetic life which fascinated early Christendom, dwells some years a hermit in the Syrian desert; till, by an apparition of magical loveliness, his life is broken up, and his nature changed: returning to the world, he embraces every vicissitude, hoping to find again the lost wisdom of that ideal beauty.

PORPHYRION

BOOK I

O from the dungeon of this flesh to break
At last, and to have peace, Porphyrion cried.
Inly tormented, as with pain he toiled
Before his dwelling in the Syrian noon:
The desert, idly echoing, answered him.
Had not the desert peace? All empty stood
That region, the swept mansion of the wind.
Pillars of skiey rock encompassed it
Afar; there was no voice, nor any sound
Of living creature, but from morn to eve
Silence abounding, that o'erflowed the air
And the waste sunshine, and on stone and herb
The tinge and odour of neglected time.

Yet into vacancy the troubled heart
Brings its own fullness: and Porphyrion found
The void a prison, and in the silence chains.

He in the unripe fervour of sweet youth
Hearing a prophet's cry, had fled from mirth
And revel to assuaging solitude.

He turned from soft entreaties, he unwound
The arms that would have stayed him, he denied
His friends, and cast the garland from his brow.
Pangs of diviner hunger urged him forth
Into the wild; for ever there to lose
Love, hate, and wrath, and fleshly tyrannies,
And madness of desire: tumultuous life.
Full of sweet peril, thronged with rich alarms.
Dismayed his soul, too suddenly revealed:
And far into the wilderness, from face
And feet of men he fled, by memory fierce
Pursued; till in the impenetrable hills
He deemed at last to have discovered peace.
Three years amid the wilderness he dwelt.
In solitary, pure aspiring turned
Toward the immortal Light, that all the stars
Outshines, and the frail shadow of our death
Consumes for ever, and sustains the sun.
The voiceless days in pious order flowed.
Calm as the gliding shadow of a cloud
On Lebanon; morn followed after morn
Like the still coming of a stream: his mind
Was habited in silence, like a robe.

Then gradually mutinous, quenched youth
Swelled up again within him, hard to tame.

For like that secret Asian wave, that drinks
The ever-running rivers, and holds all
In jealous wells; so had the desert drunk
All his young thoughts, wishes, and idle tears.
Nor any sigh returned; but in his breast
Sweet yearnings, and the thousand needs that live
Upon the touch of others, impulses
Quick as dim buds are to the rain and light,
Falterings, and leanings backward after joy,
And dewy flowerings in the heart, that make
Life fragrant, were all sealed and frozen up.
Now, at calm evening, the just-waving boughs
Of the lone tree began to trouble him:
Almost he had arisen, following swift
As after beckoning hands. Now every dawn
At once disrobed him of tranquillity:
Fever had taken him; and he was wrought
Into perpetual strangeness, visited
By rumours and bright hauntings from the world.
And now the noon intolerable grew:
The very rock, hanging about him, seemed
To listen for his footfall, and the stream
Commented, whispering to the rushes. Ah,
The little lizard, blinking in the sun.
Was spying on his soul! A terror ran
Into his veins, and he cried out aloud,
And heard his own voice ringing in the air,
A sound to start at, echoing fearfully.
He paced with fingers clenched, with knotted brow:
He cast himself upon the ground, to feel
His wild breast nearer the impassive earth.
So far away in peace, but all in vain!
And springing up he cast swift eyes around
Like a sore-hunted creature that must seek
A path to fly: alas, from his own thoughts
What outer wilderness shall harbour him?
Then after many idle purposes,
And such vain wringing of the hands, as use
Men slowly overtaken by despair,
He sought in toil, last refuge, to forget:
And he began to labour at the plot
Before his rocky cell, digging the soil
With patience, and the sweat was on his brow.
All the lone day he toiled, until at last
He rested heavy on the spade, and bowed
His head upon his hands: a shadow lay
Beneath him, and deep silence all around.
The silence seized him. As a man who feels

Some eye upon him unperceived, he turned
His head in fear: and lo, a little sound
Among the reeds, like laughter, mocked at him.
And he discerned bright eyes in ambush hid
Beyond the bushes; and he heard distinct
A song, borne to him with the clapping hands
Of banqueters; an old song heard afresh.
That melted quivering in his heart, and woke
Delicious memory: all his senses hung
To listen when that voice sang to his soul:
Then, fearfully aware, he shuddered back;
Yet could not shake the music from his ears.
He cast the spade down, with quick-beating heart,
And sought that voice, whence came it; but the reeds
In the soft-running stream were motionless,
The bushes vacant, all the valley dumb:
And clear upon the yellowed region burned
Evening serene. Then his sore troubled heart
With a tumultuous surging in his breast
Heaved to the calm heaven in a bitter cry:
I have no strength, I have no refuge more.
Father, ere thou forsake me, send me peace!

Scarce had the sun into his furnace drawn
The western hills, whose molten peaks shot far
Over the wide waste region fiery rays,
When swiftly Night descended with her stars:
And lo, upon this wrought, unhappy spirit
At last out of the darkness, raining mild
In precious dew upon the desert, peace
Incredibly descended with the night.
He stood immersed in the sweet falling hush.
Over him liquid gloom quivered with stars
Appearing endlessly, as each its place
Remembered, and in order tranquil shone.
Easily all his fever was allayed:
And as a traveller strained against a storm
That meets him, buffeting the mountain side,
Suddenly entering a deep hollow, finds
Magical ease over his nerves, and thinks
He never tasted stillness till that hour;
So eager he surrendered and relaxed
His will, persuaded sweetly beyond hope.

Tranquil at last, his solitary cell
He entered, and a taper lit, that shed
Upon rude arches and deep-shadowed walls
A clearness, tempering all with gentle beam.

Then he, that with such anguish of desire
Had supplicated peace, now peace was come.
Of all forgetful save of his strange joy.
That dear guest in his bosom, entertained;
From trouble and from the stealing steps of time
Sequestered; housed within a blissful mood
Of contemplation, like a sacred shrine;
And poured his soul out, into gratitude
Released: how long, there was no tongue to tell,
Nor was himself aware; no warning voice
Admonished, and the great stars altered heaven
Unnoted, and the hours moved over him,
When on his ear and slowly into his soul
Deliciously distilling, stole a sigh.
O like the blossoming of peace it seemed,
Or like an odour heard; or as the air
Had mirrored his own yearning joy in speech,
A whisper wandering out of Paradise.
Porphyrion, Porphyrion! Like a wind
Shaking a tree, that whisper shook his heart.
Keen to reality enkindled now
His inmost fibre was aware of all:
Vast night and the unpeopled wilderness
Around him silent; in that solitude
Himself, and near to him a human sigh!

Immediately the faint voice called again:
Thou only in this perilous wilderness
Hast found a refuge; ah, for pity's sake
Open! It is a woman weak and lost
In this great darkness, that importunes thee.

Then with a beating heart, Porphyrion spoke.
O woman, I have made my soul a vow
To look upon a human face no more.

Yet in some corner might I rest my limbs
That are so weary with much wandering,
And thou be unhurt by the sight of me!

Sweet was the voice: doubting, he answered slow.
Thou troublest me. I know not who thou art
That com'st so strangely, and I fear thy voice.
What wouldst thou with me? Enter: but my face
Seek not to meet.

Then he unclosed the door,
But turned aside, and knelt apart, and strove

Again to enter the sweet house of peace.
Yet his heart listened, as with hurried feet
The woman entered; and he heard her sigh.
Like one that after peril breathes secure.
Now the more fixedly he prayed; his will
Was fervent to be lost in holy calm,
So hardly new-recovered: but his ear
Yearned for each gentle human sound, the stir
Of garments, moving hand or heaving breast.
Amid his prayer he questioned, who is this
That wanders in this wilderness alone?
And, as he thought, the faint voice came to him:
I hunger.

Then, as men do in a dream,
Obeying without will, he sought and found
Food from his store, and brought, and gave to her.
But as he gave, he touched her on the hand:
He looked at unawares, then turned away;
And dared with venturing eyes to look again;
And when he had looked, he could not look elsewhere.
O what an unknown sweetness troubled him!
He gazed: and as wine blushes through a cup
Of water slowly, in sure-winding coils
Of crimson, the pale solitude of his soul
Was filled and flushed, and he was born anew.
Instantly he forgot all his despair
And anguished supplications after peace.
Not peace, but to be filled with this strange joy
He pined for, while that lovely miracle
His eyes possessed, nor wonder wanted more.
At last his breast heaved, and he found a voice.

Mystery, speak! O once again refresh
My famished ear with thy sweet syllables!
Thou comest from the desert night, all bloom!
I fear to look away, lest thou shouldst fade.
Art thou too moulded out of simple earth
As I, or only visitest my sight.
Deluding? Ah, Delusion, breathe again
The music of thy voice into my soul!

As if a rose had sprung within his cell
And magically opened odorous leaves,
So felt he, as she raised her eyes on him
And spoke.

Hast thou forgotten then so soon?

Hast thou not vowed never again to look
On face of woman or of man? Remember
Ere it be lost, thy vow, thy treasured vow.
O turn away thy wonder-wounded eyes,
Call back thy rashly wandering looks, unsay
Thy words, and this frail image from thy breast
Lock harshly out! Defend thy soul with prayers.
Nor hazard for a dream thy holy calm;
Lest thou repent, and this joy shatter thee.

While thus she spoke, the stirring of her soul.
Even as a breeze is seen upon a pool.
Appeared upon her face. Like the pale flower
Of darkness, the sweet moon, that dazzles first
And then delights, unfolding more and more
Her beauty, shining full of histories
On the dark world, upon Porphyrion now
She shone; and he was lifted into air
Such as immortals breathe, who dwell in light
Of memory beginningless, and hope
Endless, and joy old and forever fresh.
He heard, yet heard not, and still gazing, sighed:

Pour on, delicious Music, in my ears
Thy sweetness: for I parch, I am athirst.
Three years have I been vacant of all joy,
Have mocked my sense with famine, and the sound
Of wind and reed: but in thy voice is bliss.
How am I changed, since I have looked on thee!
Thou art not dream. Yet, if a vision only.
Tell me not yet, suffer me still to brim
My sight to overflowing, to rejoice
My heart to melting, even to despair.
Thou art not dream! Yet tell me what thou art.
That in this desert venturest so deep?

Seek not, she answered, what I am, nor whence
I come; in destiny, perhaps, my hand
Was stretched toward thee, and my way prepared.
Only rejoice that thou didst not refuse
Help to the helpless, and hast succoured me.

As the awakened earth beholds the sun.
Her saviour, when his beam delivers her
From icy prison, and that annual fear
Of death, Porphyrion in his bosom felt
Pangs of recovered ecstasy, old thoughts
Made young, and sweet desires bursting his heart

Like the fresh bursting of a thousand leaves.
Uplifted into rapture he exclaimed:

O full of bliss, out of the empty world
That comest wondrous, I will ask no more.
Enough that thou art here, that I behold
Thy face, and in thee mirrored all the world
Created newly: Eyes, my oracles,
What days, what years of wonder ye foretell!

As in a dewdrop all the morning shines
I see in you time glorious, grief refreshed,
And Fate undone.

Seest thou only this?
She said, and earnestly regarded him:
Art thou so eager after joy? Yet think
In what a boundless wilderness of time
We wander brief! Art thou so swift to taste
Of thy mortality? Yet I am come
To bring thee tidings out of every sea;
Not pearls alone, but shipwrecks in the night
Unsuccoured, and disastrous luring fires,
And tossings infinite, and peril strange.
O wilt thou dare embark? Dost thou not dread
This ocean, in whose murmur seems delight?
Will even thy hunger drive thee through the waves
To bliss? I look on thee, and see the joy
Rise up within thy bosom, and I fear.
So fragile is this sweetness, and so vast
The world: O venturous, glad voyager,
Be sure of all thy courage, for I see
Far ofF the cloud of sorrow, and bright spears,
And dirges, and joy changed from what it seemed.
Art thou still fervent, O impetuous one?
Still hastest thou to fly tranquillity?

But he on whom she looked with those deep eyes
Of bright compassion, answered undismayed:

Let me drink deep of this fountain of bliss!
Speak not of mortal fear, speak not of pain.
Thou painest, but with joy. Thou art all joy;
And in the world I have no joy but thee.
O that I had the wasted days once more
Since to this idle, barren wilderness
I fled, in fear of the tumultuous world,
Enamoured of the silence: here I dreamed

In lonely prayer to satiate my soul.
But now, I want. Rain on my thirsty heart
Thy charm, and by so much as was my loss
By so much more enrich me. I have stript
My days, imprisoned wandering desires,
Made of my mind a jealous solitude.
Pruned overrunning thoughts, and rooted up
Delight and the vain weeds of memory,
Imagining far off to capture peace.
Blind fool! But O no, let me rather praise
Foreseeing Fate, that kept so fast a watch
Over my bliss, and of my heart prepared
A wilderness to bloom with only thee!

Even now he would embrace her; but awhile
She with delaying gesture stayed him still.
Wistfully doubting, and perusing well
His inmost gaze and his adoring heart.

As from bright water on some early morn.
Under a beautiful dim-branching tree,
A gleam floats up among the leaves, and sends
Light into darkness wavering: from the light
Of his enraptured face a radiance shone
Into the mystery of her eyes; at last
To his warm being she resigned her soul.
She on his heart inscribed for evermore
Her look in that deep moment, and her love.
At unawares this trembled from her lips:

O joyful spirit, I too have need of thee!
And now he seemed to fold her in his arms,
And on the mouth to kiss her; close to him.
Surely her swimming eyes were dim with love,
Her lips against him murmured tenderly.
And her cheek touched his own: yet even now,
Even as her bosom swelled within his arms,
As like the inmost richness of a rose
Wounding, the perfume of her soul breathed up
An insupportable joy into his brain,
Even now, alas! faltering in ecstasy.
His arms were emptied; back he sank; despair
Drowned him; upon his sense the darkness closed;
And with a cry, lost in a cloud, he fell.

BOOK II

Slumber these desolated senses guard
With silence interposed and dimness kind;
While in tumultuous ebb joy and dismay
Murmur, re-gathering their surge afar.
Idle thou liest, Porphyrion, and o'erthrown
By violent bliss into a trance as deep:
Yet even in thy trance thou takest vows,
Thou burnest with a dedicated fire,
And thou canst be no more what thou hast been.
A rebel, thou wert in strong bonds, who now
Art chosen and consenting: and prepared
Is all thy path, that no more leads to peace.
But to repining fever; pain so dear,
It will not be assuaged. Awaiting thee
Is all that Love of the deep heart requires;
The ecstasy, the loss, the hope, the want
The prick of grief beneath the closed eyelid
Of him whom memory visits, but not rest;
The sweetness touched, for ever perishing
Out of the eager hands. Invisibly
Perhaps even now on thy unconscious cheek
Thy Guide is gazing, and to pity moved
He thy forgetful term gently extends.

At last from heavily unclouding sleep
Porphyrion stirs: dimly over his brain
Returns the noon, and opens wide his eyes.
Some moments by the veiling sense of use
Delayed in wonder, troubled he starts up.
Instantly he remembered; and all changed
Appeared his cell, the silence and the light:
She, whom his heart had need of, was not there.
And eager from his dwelling he came forth,
If there were sign of her. But all was still.

Suspended over the forsaken land.
The sun stood motionless, and palsied Time,
Helpless to urge his congregated hours.
Leaned heavy on the mountain: the steep noon
Had all the cool shade into fire devoured.
Then quailed Porphyrion. Lost was his new joy,
An apparition frail as a bright flame
Seen in the sun: irrevocably lost
The old thoughts that so long had sheltered him.
The fear, that presaging the heavy world
Makes wail the newborn child, he now, a man.
Thrice competent to suffer, felt afresh,

To cruel truth re-born, a naked soul.
Now he had eyes to see and ears to hear.
And knew at last he was alone: the sky
Absorbed he saw, the earth with absent face.
The water murmuring only to the reeds.
Unconscious rock, and sun-contented sand.
And even as within him keener rose
Longing unloosed, so much the heavier grew
The intensity of solitude around.

Melancholy had planned her palace here.
Dead columns, to support the burning sky,
For living senses insupportable.
She made, and ample barrenness, wherein
To ponder of defeated spirits, quenched
Desire, o'ertaken hope, courage undone,
Implored oblivion, and reje6led joy:
Nor this alone, but idleness so vast
As even the stormiest enterprise becalmed,
Till it was trivial to advance one foot
Beyond the other; rashness to provoke
An echo, where if ever man could laugh,
Laughter had seemed the end of vanity,
Were not a vanity more vain in tears.
For from the blown dust to the extremest hills,
Audible silence, that sustained despair,
A ceiling over all immovable.
Presided; and the desert, nourishing
That silence, listened, jealous of a sound
Younger than her unageing solitude;
The desert, that was old when earth was young.

Wailing into the silence, that rang back
A wounded cry, to the unhearkening ear
Of the austere ravines perhaps not strange.
The youth in that vain region stood, and cast
Hither and thither seeking, his sad eyes.

Out of the dreadful light to his dim cell
He fled for refuge. Here he had possessed
Joy, for a brief space, here She looked on him.
Here had her heart beat in her bosom close
Against his own. Her voice was in his ear;
And suddenly his soul was quieted.

Surely the visitation of such spirits
Comes not of chance, he murmured, but of truth.
Surely this was the shadow of some light

That shines, the odour of some flower that blooms,
And far off mid the great world dwells in flesh
That blissful spirit, and bears a human name.
If she be far, yet have I all my days
For seeking, and no other joy on earth:
I will arise, and seek her through the world.

With this resolve impassioned and inspired.
His thoughts were bright, and his hot bosom calmed.
Sweet was it to behold that radiant goal.
Though far, and hazardous and wide the way.
The greatness of his quest found answer in him
Of greatness, and the thousand teasing cares
That swarm upon perplexity, flew off.
Gladly against his journey he prepared
His pilgrim's need, and laid him down and slept,
And ere the dawn with scrip and staff arose.

Now at his door, irrevocably free.
Before the unknown world, spread dim and vast,
He stood and pondered, gazing forth, which way
To follow, and what distant city or vale
Held his desire; but pondering he was drawn
Forth by some secret impulse; he obeyed,
Not doubting; toward the places of his youth
He turned his face, toward the high mountain slopes
Of the dim west, and Antioch and the sea.
Up the long valley, by the glimmering stream
He went; and over him the stars grew pale.
Cliffs upon either hand in darkness plunged
Built up a shadow; but far off, in front,
Invaded by the first uncertain beam,
Mountain on mountain like a cloud arose.
He seemed ascending some old Titan stair,
That led up to the sky by great degrees,
In the vast dawn; he journeyed eagerly.
Foot keeping pace with thought; for his full heart
Tarried not, but was with its happy goal.
One face, one form, one vision, one desire.

Due onward over the unending hills
He held his way, and the warm morning sprang
Behind him, and a less impatient speed
Drove his feet onward. In the midday heat
He rested weary; and relaxing thought.
Had leisure to perceive where he had come

Burning beneath the solitary noon

All round him rose, rock upon rock o'erhung,
A fiery silence: undefended now
By clouding grief, nor in illusion armed,
He to the heavy lure all open lay
That from this mortal desolation breathed.
Out of his heart he sought to summon up
The vision, but it fled before his thought.
Only the hot blank everywhere opposed
His spirit, and the silent mountain wall.
Like one, on whom the fear of blindness comes.
For whom the sun begins to fall from heaven,
And the ground darkens, he rose up and fled.
Grasping his staff; and fearful now to pause
In that death-breathing region, onward ran.

Yet was not peril past. He had not come
Far, when his agitated eyes beheld,
Amid the uneven crumbling ground, a stone
Square-hewn and edgeways fallen; and he knew
That he had come where men long since had been.
And as he lifted up his eyes, all round
Were massy granite pillars half o'erthrown.
Propping the air; and yellow marble shone.
Dimly inscribed, fragments of maimed renown.
Over the ruined region he stole on.
Threading the interrupted clue of roads
That led all to oblivion, trenches choked
With weed, and old mounds heaped on idle gold.
And now Porphyrion paused, inhaling fast
Odours of buried fame: as in a dream,
All that remote dead city and her brisk streets,
Re-peopled and for mountain battle armed.

He apprehended. The deep wave of time
Subsiding, had disclosed englutted wrecks,
Which now so long slept idle, that they seemed
To emulate the agelessness of earth;
Did not the fondness of mortality-
Still haunt them, and a kind of youth forlorn,
As if the Desert their brief fable, man,
Indulging from austerest indolence.
Forbore a just disdain.

Porphyrion,
With beating pulses, and with running blood,
Alone on ashes perishably breathed.
As he who treads the uncertain lava fears
Each moment that his rash foot may awaken

Fire from beneath him, from that sepulchre
Of smouldering ages fearfully he fled.
And sometimes he looked backward, lest his feet
Startle a shadowy population up
In the deserted sunlight, faces stern
Of fleshless kings, to claim him for their own:
So frail appeared the heaving of his breath.
So brief his pace, so idle his desire.

At last beyond the scarred gray walls he came.
And gladly found the savage rock once more
Beneath him, nor yet dared to rest or pause.
But onward pressed, over the winding sides
Of pathless valleys, where an echoing stream
Ran far below; and ridges desolate
He climbed, and under precipices huge
And down the infinite spread slopes made way.
The eagle steering in the upper winds,
As, balanced out of sight, his eye surveyed
From white Palmyra to Damascus, flushed
Among faint-shining streams, saw him afar
Journey a shadow never wearying
From hour to hour: until at last the hills
Less steep opposed him, toward the distant plains
Declining in great uplands dimly rolled.
Here were few stubborn trees, by sunset now
With sullen glory lighted rich, till night
Rose in the east, and hooded the bare world.

Porphyrion had ascended a last ridge
Of many, and his eyes gazed out afar
On boundless country darkening; he lay down
At last, full weary: the keen foreign air
Filled his delighted nostril: and his heart
Was soothed. As on a troubled mere at night
Wind ceases, and the gentle evening brings
Beauty to that vext mirror, and all fresh
In perfect images the lost returns;
Serenely in his bosom rose anew
The vision: somewhere in that distant world,
He mused, is she; and there is all my joy.

But evening now before his gazing eyes
Receded dim, until the whole wide earth
Appeared a cloud. Then in the gloom a dread
Came whispering, and hope faltered in his breast:

O if the great world be but fantasy-

Raised by the deep enchantment of desire,
And melt before my coming like a cloud!
Parleying with the ghost of fear, yet still
Cherishing his thought's treasure, he resigned
His senses to the huge and empty night,
When on the infinite horizon, lo!
Sending a herald clearness, upward stole
Tranquil and vast, over the world, the moon.

Delicately as when a sculptor charms
The ignorant clay to liberate his dream,
Out of the yielding dark with subtle ray
And imperceptible touch she moulded hill
And valley, beauteous undulation mild,
Inlaid with silver estuary and stream,
Until her solid world created shines
Before her, and the hearts of men with peace.
That is not theirs, disquiets: peopled now
Is her dominion; she in far-off towns
Has lighted clear a long-awaited lamp
For many a lover, or set an end to toil.
Or terribly invokes the brazen lip
Of trumpets blown to Fate, where men besieged
For desperate sally buckle their bright arms.
All these, that the cheered wanderer on his height
In fancy sees, the lover's secret kiss.
The mirth-flushed faces thronging through the streets,
And ships upon the glimmering wave, and flowers
In sleeping gardens, and encounters fierce.

And revellers with lifted cups, and men
In prison bowed, that move not for their chains,
And sacred faces of the newly dead;
All with a mystery of gentle light
She visits, and in her deep charm includes.

BOOK III

Dawn in the ancient heavens over the earth
Shone up; but in Porphyrion's bosom rose
A brighter dawn: the early ray that touched
His slumber, woke the new, unfathomed need,
Fallen from radiant night into his soul.
That thirsted still for beauty; for that joy
Beyond possession, ever flying far
From our dim utterance, beauty causing tears.

He stretched his arms out to the golden sun.
His glorious kin, impetuously glad.
And with aerial morning journeyed on
O'er valley and o'er hill.

The second dawn
Found him far-travelled over pastoral lands.
Where from the shepherds' lonely huts a smoke
Went up, or some white shrine gleamed on a height.
Soon the dark ranging and unchanging pines
Yielded to ash and chestnut; O how fair
Their perishable leaf! Porphyrion knew
That some great city neared him, and his pace
Grew eager, climbing a soft-crested hill
In expectation; yet all unprepared
At last upon his eye the prospect broke,
Dawning serene, and endlessly unrolled.

There lay the city, there embodied hope
Rose to outmatch desire: he cried aloud.
Taken with joy so irresistible,
That he must seize a sapling by the stem
To uphold him, and in ardent silence gazed.
Solitary heaven, strown with vast white clouds,
Moved toward him over the abounding land;
A land of showers, a land of quivering trees,
A land of youth, lovely and full of sap,
Upon whose border trembled the wide sea.
Young were the branches round him, in fresh leaf
Luminously shaded; the arriving winds
Broke over him in soft aerial surge;
For him the grass was glittering, the far cloud
Loosened her faltering tresses of dim rain,
And broad Orontes interrupted shone.
But mid that radiant amphitheatre
He saw but the far city: thither ran
His gaze, and rested on her, in a bloom
Of distant air apparelled, while his heart
Beat at the thought of what she held for him
Bright Antioch! From the endless ocean wave
Gliding the sunbeam broke upon her towers,
A moment gleaming white, then into shade
Withdrawn, until she seemed a thing of breath.
Created fair, from whose far roofs arose
Soft, like an exhalation, human joy.

Clear as a pool to plunge in, seemed the world

This blissful morn, to him that thither gazed,
Wondering, until unconscious tears were wet
Upon his flushing cheek, while he sent forth
His eager thoughts flying to that sweet goal,
And conjuring wishes waved unknown delight
To come to him. Already in dream arrived,
Close to his ear the hum of those far streets
He hears; already sees the busy crowd
Pass and repass, with laughter and with cries,
Meeting him, children hand in hand from school
Gleefully run, and old men, slow of step,
Approach; the mason, pausing from his toil
Under the plank's cool shadow, looks at him,
Or, with a negligent wonder glancing down,
Beautiful faces; O, perhaps the face
That to his fate he follows through the world,
That deepest hope, too dear to muse upon,
A moment filled him with a thrilling light:
And as a bird, alighting on a reed
Sprung straight and slender from a lonely stream,
Some idle morning, delicately sways
The mirrored stem, and sings for perfect joy;
So musical, alighted young desire
Upon his heart, that trembled like the reed.

Down from that height, over delicious grass,
Amid the rocks, amid the trees, he sped,
The browsing sheep upstarted in the sun,
Scared by his coming; he ran on, and tore
A fresh leaf in his mouth, or sang aloud
Out of his happy heart; such keen delight
His eye was treasuring, that welcomed all
The variable blooms in the high grass,
Borage and mullein and the rust-red plume
Of sorrel, and the sprinkled daisies white,
Even the sap in the young bough he felt
Reach warmly up to the inviting sun,
As if his own blood by the spring renewed
Were theirs, and budding leaves within his breast.

At last, ere he perceived it, he was close
Upon the city walls: through shading boughs
Across a valley they rose populous
With crowding towers and roofs of distant hum.
Then in the midst of joy he was afraid.
So close to him the richness he desired
Dismayed his spirit, that to doubt and fear
Recoiling fell. Not yet will I go up,

He thought; but when the dark comes, I will go.
Even as his purpose was relaxed, his limbs
To sudden heaviness surrendered: down
He laid him in sweet grass beside a pool.
Under a chestnut, opposite a grove
Of cypress; and at once sleep fell on him:
Deep sleep, that into dark unfathomed wells
Plunges the spirit, and with ignorance lost
Acquaints, and inaccessible delight.
And unborn beauty.

But meanwhile the noon
Had ripened and grown pale in the soft sky.
A gentle rain fell as the light declined;
And, the drops ceasing, an unprisoned beam
Out of a cloud flowed trembling o'er the grove
And ran beside long shadows of the stems.
And lighted the dark underleaves, and touched
The sleeper; suddenly his cheek was warm:
He stirred an arm, and unrelaxing, sighed;
And now, through crimsoned eyelids, on his brain
The full sun burned; to wonder he awoke.
Green over him, in mystery o'erhung.
Was dimness fluttered with a thousand rays;
Unfathomable green; that living roof
A single stem upbore, whose mighty swerve
Upward he followed, till it branched abroad
In heaven, and through the dark leaves shone remote.
Smooth-molten splendour, the broad evening cloud.
Porphyrion upon his elbow leaned
And hearkened, for the trembling air was hushed
By hundred birds, praising the peaceful light
Invisibly: a wet drop from the leaf
Spilled glittering on his hand. Then he reclined
Deep into joy, absolved out of himself,
The while the wind brought to him light attired
In fragrance, and the breathing stillness seemed
Music asleep, too lovely to be stirred.

As thus he drew into his pining heart
Such juices as make young the world, and feed
The veins of spring; as into one pure sense
Embodied, he was hearkening blissfully,
A sound came to him wonderful, like pain,
With such a sweetness edged. It was a voice,
A happy voice: and toward it instantly
The fibre of his flesh yearningly turned.
Trembling as at a touch. Then he arose

Troubled: he looked, and in the grove beyond
That peaceful water, lo! a little band
Of youths and maidens under distant trees
Departing: one looked backward ere she went;
And his heart cried within his breast, awaked
Suddenly into blissful hope. Alas!
With flutter of fair robes and mingled, gay,
Faint laughter, down a bank out of his view
They were all taken. Pierced with sudden loss,
And kindled, like a wild, uncertain flame.
Into a hundred joyful, wavering fears.
He gazed upon the empty grove, the pool,
And the light brimming over on fresh grass
And lonely stems: but the bereaved bright scene
No more rejoiced him. Now, to aid his wish,
Swift night upon the fading west inclined:
And he stole forward through the cypress gloom
Toward Antioch. Halting on a neighbour brow.
Afar off he beheld that company
Even now under the dim gate entering in.
He followed, and at last the darkened street
Received him, wondering, back among his kind.

Was ever haven like the dream of it
In peril? or did ever feet attain
Their goal, but still a richer rose beyond?
It was a festal night: gay multitudes
Came idly by, and no man noted him.
His seeking gaze, hither and thither drawn,
Roamed in a mirror of desires amazed,
And found, yet wanted more than it could find.
Beauty he felt around him brushing near,
And joy in others seen; but all to him.
Without the vision that his soul required.
Was idle: solitary was his heart.
And full to breaking: yet, as wounds are dulled
To the frail sense, he knew not yet his grief.
For wonder clothed it; through a veil he heard
And saw.

Thus wandering aimlessly he found
His feet upon a marble stair; in face
A porch rose; issuing was a festal sound,
That drew him onward out of the lone night.
Halting upon the threshold he gazed in.

Pillars in lovely parallel sustained
A roof of shadowed snow, enkindled warm

From torches pedestalled in order bright;
Amid whose brilliance at a banquet sat.
Crowned with sweet garlands, revellers, and cups
Lifted in laughing, boisterous pledge, or gazed
Earnest in joy, on their proud paramours.
Pages, with noiseless tripping feet, had borne
The feast aside; and now the brimming wine
From frosted flagons blushed, and the spread board
Showed the soft cheek of apricot, or glory
Of orange burning from a dusk of leaves.
Cloven pomegranates, brimmed with ruby cels.
Great melons, purpling to the frosty core,
And mountain strawberries. Beyond, less bright,
Was hung mysterious magnificence
Of tapestry, where, with ever-moving feet,
A golden Triumph followed banners waved
O'er captive arms, and slender trumpets blew
To herald a calm hero charioted.

Just when a music, melted from above.
Over the feasters flowed, and softly fixed
The listening gaze, and stilled the idle hand,
Porphyrion entered; all those faces flushed,
Lights, flowers and laughter, and the trembling wine,
And hushing melody, and happy fume
Of the clear torches burning Indian balm.
Clouded his brain with sweetness, like a waft
Of perished youth returned; those wonders held
His eyes, yet were as things he might not touch.
And, if he stretched his hand out, they would fade.

Then he remembered whom he sought. A pang
Disturbed him; eager with bright eyes inspired.
Through those that would have stayed his feet, he stole
Nearer to bliss. They all regarded him
Astonished; in their joyful throng he seemed
An apparition: darkly the long hair

Hung on his shoulders, and his form was frail.
Some cried, then all were silent; a strange want
Woke in their sated breasts, and wonder dread
Troubled them, whence had come and what required
This messenger unknown. But he passed on.
And in each woman's face with questioning gaze.
Dazzled by nearer splendour, looked, and sought.
Doubtful.

Already one, whose arm was laid

Around the shoulder of her paramour.
Stayed him, so deep into his heart she looked.
Biting her pearly necklace: in her robe
Was moonlight shivering over purple seas.
Encountering, their spirits parleyed: then
Unwillingly he drew his eyes away.
Another, clothed as in the fiery bloom
Of cloud at evening changing o'er the sun.
Backward reclining, under lids half-closed
Gazed, and a moment held him at her feet:
Until at last one turned and dazzled him,
Of whose attire he knew not, so her face
With sun-like glory drew him: he approached;
And she, presiding beauteous and adored
Queen of that perfumed feast, beckoned him on.
Her bosom heaved; the music from her ears
Faded, and from her sated sense the glow
Of empty mirth: far lovelier were in him
Sorrow and youth and wonder and desire.
Forward she leaned, and showed a vacant place
By her, and he came near, and sat him down.

Charm-stricken also, whispering, Art thou she?
She said no word, but to his shining eyes
Answered, and of the red pomegranate fruit
Gave him to eat, and golden wine to drink,
And with pale honeyed roses crowned his hair.
All marvelled, and with murmur looked on him,
As, high exalted over realms of joy.
He sat in glory, and sweet incense breathed
Of that dominion, riches in a cloud
Descending, and before his feet prepared
The world in bloom, and in his eyes the dream
Of destiny excelled, and rushing thoughts
Radiant, and beauty by his side enthroned.

BOOK IV

Love, the sweet nourishing sun of human kind,
Who with unquenchable fire inhabitest
Worlds, that would fall into that happy death
Out of their course, were not their course so fixt;
Who from the dark soil drawest up the plant.
And the sweet leaves out of the naked tree;
Whose ardent air to taste and to enjoy
All flesh desire, even of bitter pangs

Enamoured, so that this intenser breath
They breathe, and one vi6lorious moment taste
Life perfect, over Fate and Time empowered;
Leave him not desolate, Love, who to thy glory
Is dedicated, and for thee endures
To look upon the dreadful grave of joy,
Knowing the lost is lost; comfort him now.
Thy votary, who by the pale sea-shore
In the young dawn paces uncomforted.
Ah, might not sweet embraces have assuaged
The fever which had burnt him, honeyed mouth
And the close girdle of voluptuous arms?
Nor dimly fragrant hair have curtained him
From memory? Alas, too new he came
From love, too recent from that ecstasy;
And memory mocked him under the cold stars,
With finished yet untasted pleasure sad.

Flying that fragrant lure, unhappy soul,
By the dark shore he paces: and his eyes
The dawn delights not, far off in the east
Discovering the sleeping world, and men
To all their tasks arousing, while she strews
Neglected roses on the unchanging hills.
And over the dim earth and wave unfolds
Beauty, but not the beauty he desires.
To her, to her, who in the desert touched
His spirit, and unsealed his eyes, and showed
Above a new earth a new sun, and brought
His steps forth to this perilous rich world,
Stirred with ineffable deep longing now
He turned; ev'n to behold her from afar.
To touch the hem of her apparel, seemed
Sweeter ten thousandfold than absolute
Taste and possession of a lesser charm.

Where art thou? cried he. Ah, dost thou behold
My desolation and not come to me?
O ere my sick heart all delight refuse,
Return, appear! Or say in what far land
Thou lingerest, that I may seek thee out
And find thee, without whom I have no peace
Nor joy, but wander aimless in a path
Barren and undetermined o'er the world.
Wilt not thou make thy voice upon the wind
Float hither, or in dew thy secret breathe
To answer my entreaty?

The still shore
Was echoless, unanswered that sad cry.
Warm on the wave the Syrian morning stole.
Out of suspended hazes the smooth sea
Swelled into brilliance, and subsiding hushed
The lonely shore with music: such a calm
As vexes the full heart, inviting it.
Flattered with sighing pause Porphyrion's ear.
The sea hungered his spirit; he could not lift
His eyes from the arriving splendour calm
Of those broad waters, to their solemn chime
Setting his grief; and gradually vast
His longing opened to horizons wide
As the round ocean; deep as the deep sea
His heart, and the unbounded earth his road.

That inward stream and dark necessity,
Which drives us onward in the way of Time,
Moved his uncertain hesitating soul
Into its old course, and his feet set firm
To tread their due path, seeking over earth
The Wonder that made idle all things else.
He raised his brow, inhaling the wide air;
And the wind rose, and his resolve was set.

Broad on the morrow hoisting to the sun
Her sail, a ship out of the harbour stands
Bearing Porphyrion, fervent to renew
His lonely pilgrimage; to fate his way
Committed, and to guiding beams of heaven;
And careless whither bound, so the remote
Irradiated circle, ever fresh,
Glittering into infinity, lead on.

Soon the bright water and keen kiss of the air
His clouded courage cleared; uprising wind
Swelled the resisting sail, and the prow felt
The supple press of water, cleaving it;
And the foam flashed and murmured; hope again
Rose tremulous to that music's buoyant note.
Day pursued day on the blue deep, and shores
Sprang up and faded: still his gaze was cast
Forward, and followed that undying dream.

Standing at last above a harbour strange,
Inland he bent, ever with questioning heart
Expectant; and through wilderness and town
Journeyed all summer; nor could autumn tame

That urging fire; nor mid the gliding leaves
Of bare December could hope fall from him.

Ever a stranger roamed he, nor had thought
To seek a home; for him this vast desire
Was home, that fed his spirit and sheltered him
From care and time and the perplexing world.
For not beside an earthly hearth he deemed
To find her moving whom he sought, though fair
With human limbs, and clothed in lovely flesh.

Rather some visitation swift and strange
His soul awaited. When at evening's end
He rested and each fostered secret wish
Rose trembling; when the dewy yellow moon
Slowly on cypress gardens poured her light,
And from the flowery gloom and whispering
Of leaves, a hundred odours had released,
Dimly he knew that she was wandering near,
A blissful presence, scarce beyond the marge
Of his veiled senses, in a world of beams.
Or journeying through the wild forest, he saw
Her passing robe pale mid the shadowy stems
A moment shine before his quickened steps
To leave him in the deep forsaken gloom
Pining with throbbing breast and desolate eyes;
And once in the thronged market at hot noon
Heard his name spoken, and looked round on air.

So visited, so haunted, he was led
Onward through many a city of the plain
Till vaster grew the silence, and far off
The noise of men; and he began to climb
Pastoral hills that into mountains rose
Skyward, with shelving ridges sloped between
Long days apart.

And as he wound his way
Thither, from crested town to town, he heard
Rumours of war all round him, men in arms
Saw glittering in winding files, and waved
Banners, and trumpets blown. But all to him
Was distant, borne from a far alien world
Where men in ignorant vain deeds embroiled
Lost the treasure of earth and all their soul.
Onward he kept his course, nor recked of them,
Riding the solitary forest ways.

And now again it was the time of birth,
When the young year arises in the woods
From sleep, and tender leaves, and the first flower.
Old thoughts were stirring in Porphyrion's breast.
And old desires, like old wounds, flowed anew.
It was that hour of hesitating spring
When with expanded buds and widened heaven
The heart swells into sadness, wanting joy
More ample, and unnumbered longings reach
Into a void, as tendrils into air.
O now as never seemed he to have need
Of his beloved, to be with her at last,
To see her and embrace her with his arms.
And in her bosom find perpetual peace.
Scarcely aware of the bright leaves around
His path, and heedless of his way, he rode
With bridle slack and forward absent eyes.
When piercing his deep dream a groaning cry
Smote on him; he stayed still and from his horse
Dismounted, and the rough briar pushed aside.

Hard by the path, amid the trodden grass
And bloody brambles, lay a wounded man.
Friend, fetch me water, groaned he, for I die.
The spring is near, and I have crawled thus far
But get no farther, struggle how I may.
Quickly Porphyrion ran to where the spring
Gushed bubbling, and fetched water, and came back.
The dying man drank deep, and having drunk
Half rose upon his arm, and eager asked:
How went the battle? have we won or lost?
I know not whether thou be friend or foe.
But quick, tell me! I faint.

What sayest thou
Of battles? said Porphyrion; I know not
Of what thou speakest, and I fight for none.

Faintly the other with upbraiding eyes
Regarding him, made answer. Art thou young
And is the blood warm in thy body, and yet
Thou wanderest idle? But perhaps thy hand
Knows not the sword, nor thou the ways of men?

Then kindled at his heart Porphyrion spoke.
I have no need of fighting, yet my hand
Knows the sword, and my youth was trained in arms.

Take then this blade, and bind my armour on.
For over yonder hill I think even now
They fight; there is our camp; ah, bid them come
And bury Orophernes where he fell!

Even with the word he sank back and expired.
Youthful amid the soft green leaves of spring.
That over his pale cheek and purple lips
Waved shadowing.

Nearer than his inmost thought
Was then the silence to Porphyrion's heart,
As heavily he rode, bearing the sword
For token, and the helmet on his brows.
He sought for his old thoughts and found them not.
Even as when the sudden thunder breaks
A brooding sky, and the air chills, and strange
The altered landscape shines in a cold light
And they that loitered hasten on, and oft
Shiver in the untimely falling eve,
So now on this irruption of the world
Followed a sadness, and his thoughts were changed
And yearning chilled. How idle seemed his hope,
How infinite his quest! Before his mind
Life spread deserted, vacant as a mist.

So mournful rode he; when beyond a hill,
Whose height, with hanging forest interposed.
Shut off the sun, he came into the light
Over against a valley broad that sloped
Before him; and at once burst on him full
All the glory of war and sounding arms.
He thought no more, but gazed and gazed again.

Dark in the middle of the plain beneath
An army moved against a city towered
Upon a distant eminence; even now
From the gate issued troops, with others joined
New-come to aid them, and together ranked
Stood to encounter stern the foes' assault.
These upon either wing had clouded horse
In squadrons, chafing like a river curbed
By the firm wind that meets it; crest and hoof
Shone restless as the white wind-thwarted waves.

Lonely and loud a sudden trumpet blew;
And fierce a score of brazen throats replied.
The sound redoubled in Porphyrion's soul

And forward drew him; he remembered now
His errand. In that instant the ripe war
Broke like a tempest; the great squadrons loosed
Shot forward glittering, like a splendid wave
That rises out of shapeless gloom, a form
Massy with dancing crest, threatening and huge,
And effortlessly irresistible
Bursts on the black rocks turbulently abroad,
Falling, and roaring, and re-echoing; far.
So rushed that ordered fury of steeds and spears
Under an arch of arrows hailing dark
Against the stubborn foe: they from the slope
Swept onward opposite with clang as fierce:
Afar, pale women from the wall looked down.

Porphyrion saw: he was a spirit changed.
He hearkened not to memory, hope or fear,
But cast them from him violently, and swift
To fuse in this fierce impulse all regret,
To woo annihilation, or to plunge
At least in fiery action his unused
Vain life, and in that burning furnace melt
The idle vessel and re-mould it new,
Spurred his horse on into the very midst.
And loud the streaming battle swallowed him.

Just on that instant when the meeting shock
Tumultuously clashed, and cries were mixt
With glitter of blades whirled like spirted spray,
He came: and as the thundering ranks recoiled,
They saw him, solitary, flushed and young,
A radiant ghost in the dead hero's arms.

Amazement smote them; in that pause he rode
Forward; and shouting Orophernes' name
Jubilant the swayed host came after him.
Iron on iron gnashed: Porphyrion smote
Unwearied; the bright peril stilled his brain,
The terrible joy inspired him: by his side
Vaunting, young men over their ready graves
Were rushing glorious: many as they rushed
Drank violent draughts of darkness unawares.
And swiftly fell; but he uninjured fought.
Easily as men conquer in a dream
He passed through splintered spears, opposing shields
And shouting faces, and wild cries, and blood;
Till now a hedge of battle bristling sprang
All round him, and no way appeared, and dark

This way and that the rocking weight of war
Swung heavy, shields and lances interclasped.

He in his heart felt hungrier the flame
Burning for desolation, and he flushed,
Sanguine of death; the sudden starting blood
Inflamed him, drunk as with a mighty wine.
And on an instant terror from the air
Upon the foemen fell; from heart to heart
As in mysterious mirrors flashed; afar
Triumphing cries rose all at once, and death
Shone dazzling in their eyes, and they were lost.

Then on them rushed the victors glorying.
Shaken abroad the battle fiercely flowed.
Wild-scattering sudden as quicksilver stream
Spilled in a thousand drops; the electric air
Pulsed with the vehemence of strong bodies hurled
In mad pursuit, till yielding or in flight
Or fallen, the defeated armies ran
Broken, and on the wall the women wailed.

Then to their camp the victors came, and all
Followed Porphyrion wondering, and acclaimed
His triumph: he in an exultant dream
Still moved, and had no thought, but from the lips
Of bearded captains, as around their fires
That night they told of old heroic deeds,
Heard his own praise, and feasted, and afar
Drank, like an ocean wind, the air of fame.

BOOK V

Meanwhile in the surrendered city, night
Went heavy, not in feasting nor in sleep.
Proud in submission were those stubborn hearts,
And nursed through darkness thoughts of far revenge,
Mixt with the glory of their courage vain.
And now as the first beam revisited
Their sorrow, and to each his neighbour's face
Disclosed, they stood at leisure to perceive
How grimly famine on their limbs had wrought,
And on their wasted cheeks and temples worn;
And from their eyes shone desolated fire,
Inflexible resolve unstrung in the end.
They saw the sentinels with haughty pace

Trample the thresholds of their homes, and watched
In melancholy indolence all day
Soldiers upon their errands come and go.

At evening afar off a bugle blew.
Sounding humiliation and despair
To them, but triumph to their conquering foes.
Who now in bright magnificence arrayed
Their hosts to enter the dejected walls.
Feigning indifference, each man to his door
Came forth; beneath the battlemented arch
Too soon detested ensign and proud plume
They saw; the broad flag streaming to the air
Fresh flowered purples, like a summer field,
The trumpets blown, the thousand upright spears
Shining, and drums and ordered trampling feet.

But in the van of these battalions stern
All wondered to behold a single youth.
Riding unhelmeted with ardent mien.
And all about him casting his bright eyes.
Up through the thronged street triumphing he rode.
But as he passed, his radiant look, that seemed
From some far glory to have taken light,
Shining among dark faces, suffered change.
Nothing on either side but hate or woe.
Defiant or averted, sullen youth
And wasted age, all misery, smote his gaze.
As the sun's splendour leaves a mountain peak
Sinking into the west, and ashy pale
Leaves it, the sadder from that former glow,
So from Porphyrion's face the glory ebbed,
His eye grew dim, and pain altered his brow.

At last that conquering army, with the night,
Possessed the city; and a hum arose
Like busy noise of settling bees; and fires,
Kindled, shed broad into the gloom a blaze;
And there were sounds of feasting and loud mirth,
And riot late, until by slow degrees
Returned darkness and silence, and all slept.

Only Porphyrion slept not: on his bed,
Turning from lamentable thoughts in vain,
He lay. But in that stillest hour, when first
Stars fade, and mist arises, and air chills.
Quite wearied out with toil and war within,
Slumber at length fell on him; but not peace.

Scarce had he wandered in the ways of sleep
Some moments, when before his feet appeared
Solemn and in the bright attire of dreams.
She whom his waking soul so many days,
So many months, had followed still in vain,
His dearest unattainable desire.
But now she looked into his face, and saw
His grief, and met him with reproachful eyes.

What dost thou here, Porphyrion? Her grave voice
Was musical with sorrow. Faintest thou
In seeking me, thy joy, tired of the way
Because the hour is not yet come to find?
Dost thou forget what in thy desert cell
I warned thee to be perilous on thy path.
Luring of loud distraction, and delay.
The vastness of the world and thy frail heart?
Seek on, faint not, prove all things till thou find;
And still take comfort; where thou art, I am.

Her voice, that trembled in the dreamer s soul
From some celestial distance, like a breeze,
Ended: the brightness went, and he awoke.

And lo, the placid colours of the dawn
Were stealing in: he rose, and came without.

Ah, now, sweet vision, O my perfect light,
I come to thee, my love, my only truth!
It was not I, but some false clouding self
That fell bewildered in this erring way;
Or an oblivion rose from underground
To blind me; but this place of grief and blood
I leave, to follow thee for evermore.

Full of this fervent prayer, through the dim street
He went: the stillness hearkened at his heels.
Now as he passed, in chilly waftings fresh
He scented the far morning: the blue night
Thinned, and all pale things were disclosed; and now
Even in his earnest pace he could not choose
But pause a moment; for all round he saw
Faces and forms lying in shadowy sleep
Within dark porches, and by sheltering walls,
And under giant temple-colonnades.
Utterly wearied. Some in armour lay
Dewy, with forehead upturned to the dawn,
And some against a pillar leaned, with hands

Open and head thrown back; an ancient pair
With fingers clasping slumbered, by whose side
A bearded warrior moved in his dark dream
Exclaiming fiercely; and a mother pressed
Her baby closer, even in her sleep.
He gazed upon them by a charm detained.
For heavy over all their slumber weighed;
And if one lifted voice or arm, it was
As plants that in deep water idly stir
And then are still; so these, bodies entranced,
Lay under soft oblivion deeply drowned.
But, as they slept, the light stole over them
By pale degrees, and each unconscious soul
Yielded his secret: with the hues of dawn
Into that calm of faces floated up
Out of their living and profound abyss
What thoughts, what dreams, what terrors, what dumb wails!
What gleams of ever-burning funeral fires
On haunted deserts where delight had been!
Glories, and dying memories, and desires!
What sighs, that like a piercing odour rose
From the long pain of love, what beauty strange
Of joy, and sweetness unreleased, and strength
Fatally strong to bear immortal woe.
And anguish darkly sepulchred in peace.

Porphyrion gazed, and as he gazed, he wept.
For he beheld how in those spirits frail,
Slept also passions mightier than themselves,
Waiting to rend and toss them; tiger thoughts,
Ecstasies, hungers, and disastrous loves.
Violent as storms that sleep under the wave.
Vast longings cruelly in flesh confined.
And wrecking winds of madness and of doom.
He trembled; yet as knowledge, even of things

Terrible, hath power to calm and to sustain,
His soul endured that truth, and to its depth
Feared not to plunge. Now he began to love,
And to be sorrowful with a new sorrow.

What have I done, he sighed, what have I lost,
My brothers, that I have no part in you?
Yet am I of your flesh and you of mine.
Sleep for this hour hath separated you
From one another, but from me for ever.
O that I could delay with you, and bear
Your lot! or with enchanting wand have power

To raise you out of slumber into peace!
To be entwined and rooted in that life
Which brings you want of one another, pain
Borne not alone, and all that human joy,
How sweet it were to me! O you of whom,
When you awaken, others will have need,
I envy you those trusting eyes, and hands
Put forth for help: I envy all your grief.
But I am all made of untimeliness.
Necessity drives on my soul to pass
Another way; my errand is not here.
Farewell, farewell, O happy, troubled hearts!

As a blind man who feels around him move
The blest, who see, and fancies them embraced
Or feasting in each other's joyous eyes;
With such deep envy often he turned back,
Even as he went, to those unconscious forms
That slumbered. But his spirit urged him on,
With kindled heart and quickened feet: and now
He neared the shadow of the city gate,
And saw the mountains rise beyond, far off.

With longing he drew in the freshened air.
But even at that moment he perceived,
Standing before a doorway in the dawn,
A solitary woman, motionless
As cloud at evening piled in the pale east
After retreating thunder: like the ash
Of a spent flame her cheek, and in her eyes
Deep-gazing, a great anguish lay becalmed.
Coldly she looked on him, and calmly spoke
In marble accent: Enter and behold
What thou hast done!

He would have passed due on.
Following his way resolved, but like a charm
Beautiful sorrow in this grave regard
Drew him aside. He entered and beheld.

Upon a bed, unstirring and supine.
Lay an old man, so old that the live breath
Seemed rather hovering over him, than warm
Within his placid limbs; yet had he strapped
Ancient armour upon him, and unused
A heavy sword lay by him on the ground.
Dim was the room: a table in the midst
Stood empty; in the whole house all was bare.

Now when Porphyrion entered, and with him
The woman, the old man nothing perceived:
But at the sound a boy, that by the wall
Was leaning, opened wide his painful eyes.
Porphyrion with accusing heart beheld.
Then to the woman turning, of their story
He questioned: quietly she answered him.

We were four souls under a happy roof
Until your armies came. Then was our need
More cruel every day. When first our meat
Grew scarce, we sat with feigning eyes and each
The other shunned. I know not who thou art,
But if thou takest pity upon pain,
I pray that no necessity bring thee
Hunger more dear than love. With me it was
So that I dared not look upon my child
Lest I should grudge him eat. To my old father,
Whom age makes helpless as a child, my breast
As to a child I gave: and I have stood
Under the trees and cursed them that so slow
They budded for our want: the buds we tore
Ere they could grow to leaf. So passed our days.
But worse the nights were, when sleep would not come
For hunger, and the dreadful morn seemed sweet.
And if thou wonder that I weep not now
Recounting them, it is that I have borne
What carries beyond grief.

She in her tale
Spoke nothing of her husband: he lay cold
Without the city fallen; but as now
She ended, the returning thought of him
Absented her sad eyes. And suddenly
Her heart, of a strange tenderness aware,
Out of its heavy frost was melted: then
She bowed her head, and she let forth her tears.

You that have known that bitter wound, of all
The bitterest, since no courage brings it balm,
When silent all the misery of the world
Knocks at your door and you have empty hands.
You know what dart entered Porphyrion's breast.
As he beheld and heard.

But now the boy
Turning with restless body and parched lip

Sighed, Give me water! I am so thirsty, mother,
I cannot fetch the breath into my throat.

Porphyrion filled a cup and gave to him.
Deeply he drank, closing his eyes, as bliss
Were in the cold fresh drops: unwillingly
His fingers from the cup relaxed; and now
The mother spoke.

Yesterday on the walls
One of your arrows smote him, and the wound
Torments him. If thou wilt, make water warm,
I pray thee, and bind up his cruel hurt
Afresh; for my hand trembles, I am weak.
So he made water warm, and washed the wound
With careful tender hands, and ointment soft
Laid on, and in sweet linen bound it up.
Comforted then the boy put round his neck
One arm, and sighing thanks, as a child will,
With faltering hand caressed him. That fond touch
Porphyrion endured not. Are men born
So apt to misery, thought he, that even this
Is worthy thanks? Yet his wrought heart attained
Even in such slender spending of its love
A little ease.

Now, said he, I must go,
I must not longer tarry: for she calls.
Whom I am vowed to follow and to find.
But when he looked upon those three, they seemed
To need him in their helplessness; the child
Divining, mutely prayed him: he resolved
For that day to remain and then to go.

So all that day he tended them and went
Abroad into the town, and brought them food,
Bartering his share of spoil for meat and bread.
And freshest fruit, and delicatest wine;
Nor marked he as he went the frowning eyes
Of the stern soldiers, how they stood and watched
Murmuring together, sullen and askance.
As in a slumbering great city, snow
With gentle foot comes muffling empty ways.
Corners and alleys, and to the tardy dawn
Faint the murmur of toil ascends, and dumb
The wheels roll, and the many feet go hushed,
So on his mind lay sorrow: hum of arms
And voices, all were soft to him and strange.

Day passed, and evening fell, and in that house
All slept; and once again he would renew
His journey; but once more his heart perplexed
Smote him, to leave them so: They have no friend,
He said, and who will tend them, if not I?
The next day he abode, and with fond care
Ministered to their need, and still the next
Found him delaying and his own dim pain
Solacing sweetly; for the old man now
By faint degrees returned to healthful warmth,
And grave with open eyes serenely looked
In a mild wonder on this unknown friend:
The mother, taxed no longer to endure
Even to her utmost strength, permitted calm
To her worn spirit, and her wasted limbs
Resigned into a happy weariness;
And the child's hurt began to be appeased.

On the fourth morn Porphyrion arose,
And saw them all still laid in peaceful sleep.
Now, said he, will I go upon my quest.
Less troubled: they have need of me no more.
He turned to go, but in the early light
Still looked upon them, and his heart was full;
And softly he unbarred the door, and seemed
Within his soul to see the whole great world
Await his coming, and its wounded breast
Disclose, and all life radiantly unroll
Her riches, opening to an endless end.

Filled with the power of that impassioned thought,
Into the silence of the morning sun
He came; and on a sudden was aware
Of men about the entrance thronged; they set
Their bright spears forward, and his path opposed.
Astonished, he looked on them, and perceived
The faces of those warriors he had brought
Thither exulting, and in victory led;
Yet on their faces he beheld his doom.
He stood in that great moment greatly calm,
Proudly confronting them, and cried aloud:
What murmur you against me? I for you
Fought, and you triumphed. Have I asked of one
A single boon? Soldiers, will you take arms
Against your captain? Men, will you dare to strike
A man unarmed? You answer not a word!
Put up your swords; for now I will pass on

To my own work, and as I came will go.

There was a stillness as he ceased, and none
Answered, but none gave way. As when in heaven
Clouds curdle, and the heavy thunder holds
All things in stupor hushed, they stood constrained.
Menacing and mistrustful; and their hearts
Grew cruel: the uncomprehended light.
That in Porphyrion shone and flushed his brow
With radiance, like the bright ambassador
Come from an unknown power, tormented them;
And dark enchanting terror drove them on.
Then one by stealth an arrow to his bow
Fitted, and strung, and drew it, and the shaft
Beside Porphyrion in the lintel stuck
Quivering: and at once they fiercely cried.
Like the loud drop that loosens the pent storm,
That loosened arrow drew tempestuous hail
From every bow: they lusted after blood,
And put far from them pity: and he fell
Before them. Yet astonished and dismayed.
Those sacrificers saw the victim smile
Triumphing and incredulous of death.
Even in anguish: pang upon fresh pang
Rekindled the lost light, the perished bloom
Of memory, and he was lifted far
In exaltation above death; he drank
Wine at the banquet, and the stormy thrill
Of battle caught him, and he knew again
The dart of love and the sweet wound of grief
In one transfigured instant, that illumed
And pierced him, as the arrows pierced his side.
Then, mingling all those bright beams into one
Full glory, dawned upon his dying sense
She whom his feet followed through all the world
Out of the waste, and over perilous paths,
Dearer than breath and lovelier than desire.
Like the first kiss of love recovered new
Was the undreamed-of joy, that he in death
With the last ecstasy of living found,
Tasted and touched, as she embraced his soul.
Then the world perished: stretching forth his arms.
Into the unknown vastness eagerly
He went, and like a bridegroom to his bride

With beckoning fingers bright
In heaven uplifted, from the darkness wakes,
Upon a sudden, radiant Fire,
And out of slumber shakes
Her wild hair to the night;
Bewitching all to run with hurried feet.
And stand, and gaze upon her beauty dire.

For her the shrinking gloom
Yields, and a place prepares;
An ample scene and a majestic room:
Slowly the river bares
His bank; above, in endless tier.
Glittering out of the night the windows come.
To that bright summons; and at last appear.
Hovering, enkindled, and unearthly clear.
Steeple, and tower, and the suspended dome.

But whence are these that haste
So rapt? what throngs along the street that press.
Raised by enchantment from the midnight waste.
That even now was sleeping echoless:
Men without number, lured from near and far
As by a world-portending star!
Lo, on the bright bank without interval
Faces in murmuring line,
With earnest eyes that shine,
Across the stream gaze ever; on the waall
Faces; and dense along the bridge's side
Uncounted faces; softly the wheels glide
Approaching, lest they break the burning hush
Of all that multitude aflush
With secret strange desire.
Warm in the great light, as themselves afire,
Thousands are gazing, and all silently!
How to the throbbing glare their hearts reply,
As tossing upward a dim-sparkled plume,
The beautiful swift Fury scares the sky.
The stars look changed on high.
And red the steeples waver from the gloom.
Distantly clear over the water swells
The roar: the iron stanchions dribble bright,
And faltering with strong quiver to its fall,
Drops, slowly rushing, the great outer wall.
From lip to lip a wondering murmur goes.

As crouching a dark moment o'er its prey,
Swiftly again upleaps
The wild flame, and exulting madly glows;
The city burns in an enchanted day.
Still the great throng impassioned silence keeps,
Like an adoring host in ecstasy.
Did ever vision of the opened sky
Entrance more deeply, or did ever voice
Of a just wrath more terribly rejoice?
The houseless beggar gazing has forgot
His hunger: happy lovers' hands relax;
They look no more into each other's eyes.
Wrapt in its mother's shawl
The fretting child no longer cries.
And that soul-piercing flame
Melts out like wax
The prosperous schemer's busy schemes:
The reveller like a visionary gleams.
An aged wandering pair lift up their heads
Out of old memories: to each, to all,
Time and the strong world are no more the same,
But threatened, perishable, trembling, brief.
Even as themselves, an instant might destroy,
With all the builded weight of years and grief,
All that old hope and pleasant usage dear.
Glories and dooms before their eyes appear
Upon their faces joy.
Within their bosoms fear!

Is it that even now
In all, O radiant Desolation, thou
Far off prefigurest
To each obscurely wounded breast
The dream of what shall be?
And in their hearts they see
Rushing in ardent ruin out of sight
With all her splendour, with her streaming robe
Of seas, and her pale peoples, the vast globe
A sudden ember crumble into night?

MARTHA

A woman sat, with roses red
Upon her lap before her spread,
On that high bridge, whose parapet
Wide over turbulent Thames is set,

Between the dome's far glittering crest
And those famed towers that throng the west.
Neglectful of the summer air
That on her pale brow stirred the hair.
She sat with fond and troubled look,
And in her hand the roses shook.
Shy to her lips a bloom she laid,
Then shrank as suddenly afraid:
For from the breathing crimson leaf
The sweetness came to her like grief.
Dropping her hands, her eyes she raised.
And on the hurrying passers gazed.
Two children loitering along
Amid that swift and busy throng.
Their arms about each other's shoulder.
The younger clinging to the older.
Stopped, with their faces backward turned
To her: the heart within her yearned.
They were so young! She looked away:
O, the whole earth was young to-day!
The whole wide earth was laughing fair;
The flashing river, the soft air,
The horses proud, the voices clear
Of young men, frequent cry and cheer,
All these were beautiful and free.
Each with its joy: Alas, but she!
She started up, and bowed her head,
And gathering her roses fled.

Through dim, uncounted, silent days,
She had trod deep-secluded ways;
Mid the fierce throng of jostling lives.
Whom unrelenting hunger drives,
Close to the wall had stolen by;
Yet could not shun Calamity.
Her painful thrift, her patient face.
Could not the world-old debt erase;
Nor gentle lips, nor feet that glide,
Persuade the sudden blow aside.
This morn, when she arose, her store,
Trusted to others, was no more.
No more avail her years of care.
She must her bosom frail prepare,
Exposed in her defenceless age.
Against the world and fortune's rage.
For bread, for bread, what must be done?
She stole forth in the morning sun.
I will sell flowers, she thought: this way

Seemed gentler to her first dismay.

Soon to the great flower-market, fair
With watered leaves and scented air,
She came: her seeking, timorous gaze
Wandered about her in amaze.
The arches hummed with cheerful sound;
Buyers and sellers thronged around:
Lilies in virgin slumber stirred
Hardly, the gold dust brightly blurred
Upon their rich illumined snow.
As the soft breezes come and go.
From her smooth sheath, with ardent wings.
Purple and gold, the iris springs;
Deep-umbered wall-flowers, dusk between
The radiance and the odour keen
Of jonquils, this sad woman's eyes
And her o'erclouded soul surprise.
But most the wine-red roses, deep
In sunshine lying, warm asleep.
Breathing perfume, drinking light
Into their inmost bosoms bright.
Seem fathomlessly to unfold
A treasure of more price than gold.
Martha, o'ercome by wonder new.
Into her heart the crimson drew;
The colour burning on her cheek.
She stood, in strange emotion weak.
But she must buy. Her choice was made:
Red rose upon red rose she laid.
Lingering; then hastened out, with eyes
Bright, and her hands about the prize.

And quickened thought that nowhere aims.
Soon, pausing above glittering Thames,
She spreads the flowers upon her knees.
Vast, many-windowed palaces
Before her raised their scornful height
And haughtily struck back the light.
She scarcely marked them; only bent
Her fond gaze on the flowers, intent
To bind them in gay bunches, drest
So to allure the spoiler best.
But now, as her caressing hand
Each odorous gay nosegay planned,
A new grief smote her to the heart:
Must she from her sweet treasure part?
They seemed of her own blood. O no,

I cannot shame my roses so:
I will get bread some other way.
So she shut out all thought. The day
Was radiant; and her soul, surprised
To beauty, and the unsurmised
Sweetness of life, itself reproved
That had so little felt and loved!
O now to love, if even a flower.
To taste the sweet sun for an hour,
Was better than the struggle vain.
The dull, unprofitable pain.
To find her useless body bread.
Stricken with grievous joy, she fled.

She fled, but soon her pace grew faint.
She paused awhile, and easier went.
Often, in spirits wrought, despair.
Not less than joy, the end of care,
A lightness feigns: for all is done,
And certainty at last begun.
Martha, with impulse fresh recoiled
From empty years, forlorn and soiled,
Trembled to feel the radiant breeze
Blowing from unknown living seas,
And rising eager from long fast
Drank in the wine of life at last.
Now, as some lovely face went by.
She noted it with yearning eye;
She joyed in the exultant course
Of horses, and their rushing force.

At last, long wandering, she drew near
Her home; then fell on her a fear,
A shadow from the coming Hours.
By chance a hawker crying flowers
His barrow pushed along the street,
And the dull air with scent was sweet.
As on her threshold Martha stood,
A sudden thought surprised her blood.
Quickly she entered, and the stair
Ascended; first with gentle care
Cooled her tired roses: then a box
Of little hoardings she unlocks,
And brings her silver to the door
And buys till she can buy no more.

Laden she enters: the drear room
Glows strangely; the transfigured gloom

Flows over, prodigal in bloom.
Her lonely supper now she spread;
But with her eyes she banqueted.
Over the roofs in solemn flame
The strong beam of the sunset came,
And from the floor striking a glow
Burned back upon the wall; and lo!
How deep, in double splendour dyed,
Blushed the red roses glorified!
When darkness dimmed them, Martha sighed
Yet still about the room she went
Touching them, and the subtle scent
Wandered into her soul, and brought
All memories, yet stifled thought.
As in her bed she lay, the flowers
Haunted her through the midnight hours:
'Twixt her shut lids the colours crept;
But wearied out, at last she slept.

Next morning she awoke in dread.
O mad, O sinful me! she said.
What have I done? how shall this end
For me? Alas, I have no friend.
She strove to rise; but in her brain
A drowsy magic worked like pain.
She sank back in a weak amaze
Upon the pillow: then her gaze
Fell on the roses; she looked round.
And in the spell again was bound.
The deep-hued blossoms standing by
With serious beauty awed her eye;
Upward inscrutable they flamed:
Of that mean fear she was ashamed.
All day their fragrance in the sun
Possessed her spirit: one by one,
She pondered o'er them, dozing still
And waking half against her will.
Her body hungered, but her soul
Was feasting; gradually stole
The evening shadow on her bed.
She could no longer lift her head.
Deep on her brain the flowers had wrought;
Now in the dim twilight her thought
Put trembling on a strange attire,
And blossomed in fantastic fire.
She stretched her hand out in the gloom:
It touched upon a living bloom.
Thither she turned; the deep perfume

O'ercame her; nearer and more near,
And now her joy is in her fear,
The lily hangs, the rose inclines.
With incense that her soul entwines,
Her inmost soul that dares not stir.
The gentle flowers have need of her.
Unpitying is their rich desire;
Her breath, her being they require.
O she must yield! She sinks far down,
Conquered, listless, happy, down
Under wells of darkness, deep
Into labyrinths of sleep,
Perishing in sweetness dumb.
By the close enfolding bloom
To a sighing phantom kissed,
Like a water into mist
Melting, and extinguished quite
In unfathomed odorous night.

At last, the brief stars paling, dawn
Breathed from distant stream and lawn.
The earliest bird with chirrup low
Called his mates; softly and slow
The flowers their languid petals part.
And open to the fragrant heart.
And now the first fresh beam returned.
Bright through the lily's edge it burned
And filled the purple rose with fire.
And brightened all their green attire,
And woke a shadow on the wall.

But Martha slept, nor stirred at all.

THE DRAY

Dim through the darkened street
The Dray comes, rolling an uneven thunder
Of wheels and trampling feet;
The shaken windows stare in sleepy wonder.

Now through an open space,
Where loitering groups about the tavern's fume
Show many a sullen face
And brawling figure in the lighted gloom,

It moves, a shadowy force

Through misery triumphant: flushed, on high,
Guiding his easy course,
A giant sits, with indolent soft eye.

He turns not, that dim crowd
Of listless forms beneath him to behold;
Shawled women with head bowed
Flitting in hasty stealth, and children old:

Calm as some conqueror
Rode through old Rome, nor heeded at his heel,
Mid the proud spoils of war,
What woeful captives thronged his chariot wheel.

ELEONORA DUSE AS MAGDA

The theatre is still, and Duse speaks.
What charm possesses all,
And what a bloom let fall
On parted lips, and eyes, and flushing cheeks!
The flattering whisper and the trivial word
No longer heard,
The hearts of women listen, deeply stirred.
For now to each those quivering accents seem
A secret telling for her ear alone:
The child sits wondering in a world foreknown,
And the old nod their heads with springing tear,
Confirming true that acted dream.
And the soul of each to itself revealed
Feels to the voice a voice reply,
With a leaping wonder, a joy, a fear,
It is I, it is I!
But O what radiant mirror is this that dazzles me,
That my dead rapture holds,
That all my loss unfolds.
That sets my longings free.
My sighs renumbers, my old hope renews.
I have lived in a sleep, I have tasted alien bread,
I have spoken the speech, and worn the robes of the dead;
I have buried my heart away, and none believed.
But now, speak on, and my bonds untie:
At last, it is I, it is I!

MIDSUMMER NOON

At her window gazes over the elms
A girl; she looks on the branching green;
But her eyes possess unfathomed realms,
Her young hand holds her dreaming chin.

Drifted, the dazzling clouds ascend
In indolent order, vast and slow.
The great blue; softly their shadows send
A clearness up from the wall below.

An old man houseless, leaning alone
By the tree-girt fountain, only heeds
The fall of the spray in the shine of the sun.
And nothing possessing, nothing needs.

The square is heavy with silent bloom;
The tardy wheels uncertain creep.
Above, in a narrow sunlit room,
The widower watches his child asleep.

THE PARALYTIC

He stands where the young faces pass and throng;
His blank eyes tremble in the noonday sun:
He sees all life, the lovely and the strong,
Before him run.

Eager and swift, or grouped and loitering, they
Follow their dreams, on busy errands sped.
Planning delight and triumph; but all day
He shakes his head.

SONGS OF THE WORLD UNBORN

Songs of the world unborn
Swelling within me, a shoot from the heart of Spring,
As I walk the ample and teeming street
This tranquil and misty morn,
What is it to me you sing?

My body warm, my brain clear.
Unreasoning joy possesses my soul complete;
The keen air mettles my blood.

And the pavement rings to my feet.
O houses erect and vast, O steeples proud,
That soar serenely aloof.
Vistas of railing and roof,
Dim-seen in the delicate shroud of the frosty a r,
You are built but of shadow and cloud,
I will come with the wind and blow.
You shall melt, to be seen no longer, O phantoms fair.
Embattled city, trampler of dreams,
So long deluding, thou shalt delude no more;
The trembling heart thou haughtily spurnest,
But thou from a dream art sprung,
From a far-off vision of yore,
To a dream, to a dream returnest.

Time, the tarrier,
Time, the unshunnable.
Stealing with patient rivers the mountainous lends,
Or in turbulent fire upheaving,
Who shifts for ever the sands,
Who gently breaks the unbreakable barrier.
Year upon year into broadening silence weav ng.
Time, O mighty and mightily peopled city.
Time is busy with thee.
Behold, the tall tower moulders in air,
The staunch beam crumbles to earth,
Pinnacles falter and fall,
And the immemorial wall
Melts, as a cloud is melted under the sun.
Nor these alone, but alas.
Things of diviner birth,
Glories of men and women strong and fair.
They too, alas, perpetually undone!
As the green apparition of leaves
Buds out in the smile of May;
As the red leaf smoulders away,
That frozen Earth receives;
In all thy happy, in all thy desolate places,
They spring, they glide.
Unnumbered blooming and fading faces!
O what shall abide?

Aching desire, mutinous longing.
Love, the divine rebel, the challenge of all.
Faith, that the doubters doubted and wept her fall,
To an empty sepulchre thronging:
These, the sap of the earth,
Irresistibly sprung,

In the blood of heroes running sweet,
In the dream of the dreamers ever young.
Supplanting the solid and vast delusions,
Hearten the heart of the wronged to endure defeat,
The forward-gazing eyes of the old sustain,
Mighty in perishing youth, and in endless birth.
These remain.

THE SUPPER

A PROLOGUE

A rich youth invites a chance company of guests from the street — a blind beggar, a sandwich-man, a tramp, two women, and a thief all fallen in the world: they are seated at supper in a sumptuous room.

THE SUPPER

Host
Linger not, linger not, lift your glasses.
Mirth shall come, as misery passes.
Hark, how the mad wind blows his horn
And hunts the laggards in streets forlorn!
Hark, how fierce the winter rain
Beats and streams on the window pane!
Ill is it now for the houseless head,
And for him that makes on the ground his bed.
But we will forget in the warmth of the fire,
And be glad, and taste of our heart's desire.
Laugh old care and trouble down
And toils and sad remembrance drown!
All is yours; all sorrow bury
To-night, and with me for an hour be merry.

Madge
You are kind, sir.

Host
O believe you not
That it makes my joy to cheer your lot?
You see me, who have lived my days
In riches, pleasure, friendship, praise.
I was not happy, I wanted more;
To-day I have found what I missed before.
I have sought you and brought you from cold and rain;
Now I will raise you out of your pain.

And you, old man, shall be young with me,
Brisk and glad as you used to be;
And you, child, with your cheeks so white,
Shall feel fresh blood in your pulse to-night.
Linger not, linger not, eat your fill.
Drink and be merry.

All
We will, we will!

Blind Roger
Set the glass in my hand. I'm blind and old,
But still I shun to be left in the cold.

Host
Is it hard at the first to remember the way
Of mirth, and be rid of the load of the day?
O, be not afraid to laugh and to smile.

Averill
Our lips, it may be, are slow awhile.
And our hearts unused to gaiety yet.
But let us forget.

Tony
Ay, let us forget.

Michael
That 's easy, mates; but that 's the least.
Now we're set to so rare a feast,
I'm ripe and ready for all gay cheer,
But the great wax lights, so soft and clear.
Abash me, and make my eyes afraid.

Host
Wait but a moment, the dazzle will fade:
Soon to your eyes will the light be as bloom.
And your ears be filled with the peace of the room.
Were the wind but quiet, instead of the toil
And the traffic beneath, with its huge turmoil.
You'd fancy the lonely fields around.

Annie
'Tis soft and calm, but I miss the sound.

Averill
O, it is sweet for an hour to be lulled,

For an hour to be happy with senses dulled.

Tony
Ah, ah, the silver, how it gleams!
I have seen such glitterings in my dreams.

Roger
Long, long ago, when my eyes could see.
Such sweet odours used to be.

Michael
What a fruit is this to melt in the mouth!

Host
I have a garden in the South.
It brings me summer warm in frost,
Glories fallen and odours lost.
I love fresh roses in the snow;
I love them best when the leaves are low.

Annie
What wonderful colours are these that burn
In the red flower blushing beneath the fern.

Madge
How cold are your hands, lass!

Host
Come to the fire.
Come, let us heap the bright coal higher.
Now the sparks fly.

Michael
The fire is good;
The blessed red flames warm my blood.
Better this than the stars I saw
Shine last night, where I lay on the straw,
Through a chink in the roof of the mouldering shed.
Ha, ha! I thought it a famous bed,
And slept like a prince in his palace till day.
When the cursing farmer drove me away.

Tony
Once I sat in as fine a room;
The host was away, but we were at home;
We drank his health in his own red wine.
'Twas midnight when we sat to dine:
We filled our bellies, and slept for a spin.

And softly we laughed as the dawn came in.

Michael
Now we are merrier, now for a song.
O, for some music to bear it along.

Roger
I once could sing my song with the best;
I rolled my voice up out of my chest.
But the sap is dried in my bones: so you,
That have voice and blood and all things new,
Sing i with the burden we'll all come in.

Host
Moisten your mouth then, ere you begin.
I pledge you, friends. Your health! and yours

Michael
May you be merry while breath endures.

Tony
May you be merry, whatever befall.

Annie
Good luck!

Madge
Good luck!

Host
Good luck to you all!

Michael [singing]
Wander with me, wander with me:
Care to the devil, be free, be free!
Who but a fool would scrape and save,
To heap up a molehill and live in a grave?

Roger [quavering]
Wander with me, wander with me!

Michael
I saw the old landlord, the miser gray,
Gather his greedy rents to-day.
The old gray rat with fiery eyes.
He stamped with his stick and he snuffed for a prize.
Lord, how the starveling tenants shivered,
And into his ravening claws delivered.

Death pulls at his foot with a right good will;
But he fleshes his teeth with a relish still.
What prayers and excuses! I laughed to hear.
I that owed nothing, had nothing to fear.

Madge
O men are cruel! I've seen them go
And turn folks houseless into the snow.

Michael [singing]
What rent pay I to the air and the sun?
The days and the nights are mine, every one;
When I've finished with one, there 's another begun.
Wander with me, wander with me,
Care to the devil, be free, be free!

All
Wander with me, wander with me!

Michael
Yes, I tell you, sir, I tell you, my friend,
I drink your good luck, but be sure of the end.
You never can tell you won't come to the cold,
And the bed from under your body be sold.
You smile at your ease; you pay no heed;
You think to lay hands on all that you need.
And still you go piling your riches high;
But where is the use of it all, say I?

Host
Well said, my friend: you've a heart in your breast;
And a brave heart beating is worth all the rest.
Where is the use of it all? 'Tis true:
But we walk in the way we're accustomed to.

Michael
He with his riches, he dares not believe me!
With banquets and couches he thinks to deceive me.
Give me a glass of the bright stuff there;
And you, that sit so straight in your chair,
What are you thinking so sadly of, yonder,
You dreamer of dreams? To be merry and wander
Over the world, is it wiser, say,
Than to sit and grow fat and let life slip away,
Till your blood turns chill and your hair turns gray?

Averill
I think I have wandered the whole earth round,

An endless errand, nowhere bound.
I look straight, and nothing see
In the world, and no man looks on me.
What have I with men to do?
I hear them laugh, as I pass them through
In the street; I feel them stop and stare
At the boards that over my shoulder flare.
What matters my ragged and grimy coat.
My aching back, my parching throat?
I am a beacon to laughter and leisure;
I point all day the path to pleasure!

[A pause.

Madge
How strange we look in the mirror tall!
It casts a brightness about us all.
Here are we round a table set.
And until this night we had never met!

Roger
Your mirth soon flags. When I was young,
We'd have been merry the whole night long.

Michael
Ay, mates, we're wasting our pleasure. Drink'
We came not here to be sad and to think.

Madge
'Tis all day toiling that clouds the head.

Host
What do you do for daily bread?

Madge
I sell my matches along the street.
I see the young with nimble feet,
The fair and the foolish, the feeble and old.
That crawl along in the mire and the cold;
And the sound is always in my ears.

the long, long crowding, trampling years.
Since I was young and followed after
The lights, the faces, the glee, the laughter!
But now I watch them hurry and pass
As I see you all now, there in the glass.
Annie, so pale? What ails you, lass?

Annie

I am faint, I am tired; but soon 'twill go —
On the pavement I never felt it so:
All is so strange here, I am afraid.

Host

Afraid? What grief, my girl, has made
Such foolish fears come into your thought?
We are all friends: and friends or not,
None should harm you within these doors.
Outside is the world that raves and roars.
But you, I marvel how you, so slight.
Endure alone so vast a fight.

Annie

I know not how, but down in the street
'Tis not so heavy a task to meet.
A power beyond me bears me along,
The faint with the eager, the weak with the strong.
'Tis like an army with marching sound:
I march, and my feet forget the ground.
I have no thought, no wish, no fear;
And the others are brave for me. But here,
I know not why, I long to rest;
I have an aching in my breast.
O I am tired! how sweet 'twould be
To yield, and to struggle no more, and be free!

Michael

Courage, lass, hold up your head;
Never give in till its time to be dead.

Host

Nay, rest, if you will. Yet taste this wine,
The cordial juice of a golden vine.
'Twill cheer your spirit, 'tis ripe and good,
And it goes like sunshine into the blood.

Madge

Eat this fruit, too, that looks so rich,
So smooth and rosy. Is it a peach?
'Tis soft as the cheek of a child, I swear.

Annie [absently]

As the cheek of a child?

Michael

Come, never despair —

But the sad man, what is he mumbling there?

Averill
To the lost, to the fresh.
To the sweet, to the vain,
Turn again. Time,
And bring; me again.

I feel it from far
Like the scent of a leaf;
I see and I hear;
It is joy, it is grief.

What have we done
With our youth? with the flowers
With the breeze, with the sun.
With the dream that was ours?

Our thoughts that blossomed
Young and wet!
What have we drunken
Quite to forget?

Where have we buried
Our dead delight?
We could not endure it;
It shone too bright.

O it comes over me
Keener than pain.
All is yet possible
Once, once again!

[A silence.

Annie [starting up
What am I doing?
Eating and drinking!
I strangle, I choke
With the pain of my thinking.
He wants me, he cries for me,
Somewhere, my boy,
My baby, my own one joy.
They said 'twas a sin to have borne him:
My sin was to desert him.
He that hung at my breast and trusted me,
How had I heart to hurt him?
I must go, through the night, through the cold, through the rain,

I must seek, I must toil, till I find him again.

Host
Stay, stay!

Madge
O Annie, how can you bear
To tell your shame, where all can hear?

Annie
I wish that I were lying
In my love's arms again.
My body to him was precious
As now it is worthless and vain.
What matters to me what you say? Let me go.
But you, O why did you wake my woe?
I wanted not feasting, nor mirth, nor wine,
Nor the things that I know shall never be mine,
I wanted only to sleep and forget.

Host
She's gone.

Madge
The night's wild.

Averill
Wild and wet

Tony
Hark, how the wind in the chimney hums.

Averill
It beats and threatens like distant drums.

Host
Come to the fire. Fill once more
Your glasses.

Michael
It is not now as before.
The good drink tastes no longer well.

Madge
I am full of fears that I cannot tell.
Why am I weak and lonely and old?

Roger

Where is it gone? I seemed to behold
For a moment, but now, the blessed light.
Alas, again it is black, black night!

Tony
I once was loved by a lass, I see
Her smile, I hear her calling to me.
Could I feel her kiss on my mouth again —

Roger
O could I see for a moment plain!

Michael
I had a friend, he was dearer than brother.
I loved him as I loved none other.
I struck him in drink; he left me for ever.
I shall grasp his hand again never, never!

Averill
What have you done to us? Why have you brought
All sad thoughts that ever we thought,
And this evil spell around us cast?

Madge
We were all merry a moment past.

Host
What will you have, friends? What shall I do
For your comfort? What shall I give to you?

Averill
My youth!

Roger
My sight!

Tony
My love!

Michael
My friend!

Madge
O make me sure of peace in the end.

Host
I gave you freely of all I had,
It is not my doing, you are not glad.

Averill
We want.

Tony
We hunger.

Averill
Ah, once more
Let us hope, let us love, let us live.

Michael
Restore
What we have lost, what you possess.
You that are stronger for our distress.
You that have wakened our hearts this day.

Host
My friend, you know not what you say.

Roger [in a low voice]
Why did he ask us hither to-night?

Madge
And question, too, of our evil plight?

Tony
Why did he drive us to be glad?

Roger
To make us remember what once we had.

Madge
Youth and happiness well forgot!

Tony
To spy on our trouble.

Michael
A devil's plot!
Damn the poison! Drink no more!
I wish I had spilt my glass on the floor
Ere I made merry with him. His guest!
To watch us befooled, 'twas an excellent jest!

Roger
I wish I could see his face.

Michael

He stands,
Pale and angry, with twitching hands.
O his sport is spoiled; he's vext to know
That we've found him out.

Madge

Let us go, let us go.

Michael

Ay, we've our pride, as well as he.
Come out to the street, in the street we are free.

Tony

Curse the light that dazzled our eyes!

Michael

Curse the drink that taught us lies!

Madge

Say no more, but let's begone.

Roger

Curse the mocker that lured us on!

Michael

May your pleasure perish, your grief increase.
Your heart dry up.

Averill [breaking in]
Peace, friends, peace.

Host [astonishedy and struggling with himself].
Ungrateful!

Averill

You know not, sir, perchance,
How misery turns the mind askance.

Host

I pitied you.

Averill

Pity, sir, 'tis well,
But it will not hold men up from hell.
Silence, friends: you have had your way.
Now 'tis for me to say my say.
Listen well, our host: my youth

Comes back; I burn with the fire of the truth.
It lights my thoughts and kindles my tongue;
And he must speak, whose heart is wrung.

Behold us, who ask not pity,
We were not what we are;
For a moment now we remember:
O, we have fallen far!

We are Necessity's children.
Our Mother, that bore us of old.
Has her mark on us all: she brings us
All, in the end, to her fold.

We have wandered in meadow and sun;
But she calls us up from the flowers.
She is our will, our purpose;
The aching flesh is ours.

Hark, in the lulling tempest,
Close on the wild wind's heels.
The sound that makes men tremble,
The sound of her chariot wheels!

She calls. We must not tarry.
We must take up our yoke again,
With labouring feet for ever
To follow her triumph's train;

To follow her sleepless course,
And to fall when she decrees
With wailings that no man hearkens,
With tramplings that no man sees.

With the great world glorying round us.
As the dying soldier hears.
Far off in the ebb of battle.
His conquering comrades' cheers.

Is your heart grown tender toward us?
Would you lift us up from the mire?
Would you set our feet in the way
To follow our far desire?

O, you must have strength to fashion
Our bones and bowels anew.
With fresh blood fill these bodies.
Ere we may have part with you.

Farewell, for our Mother calls:
We go, but we thank you, friend.
Who have lifted us up for a moment.
To behold our beginning and end.

We are clothed with youth and riches,
We are givers of feasts to-night,
We spread our plenteous table
And heap it in your sight.

You need not to sharpen hunger;
All shall be well appeased.
If you find our fare to your pleasure,
You shall depart well pleased.

Have you tasted a relish keener
Than the pang of useless pain?
Know you a spice more rare
Than the tears of wisdom rain?

Come, eat of the mad desires
That rend us we know not why.
The terrors that hunt us, the torment
That will not let us die.

Taste, it is ripe to bursting.
The sorrow-scented fruit.
That weakness sowed in darkness,
That found in the night its root.

That blossomed in great despairs.
And is trodden to earth in scorn.
By the ignorant feet that trample
The faces of babes unborn.

The laughter of men that mock,
The silence of women that fear.
The shrinking of children's hands:
Come taste, all these are here.

Drink, drink of the blood-red wine,
That the smilers and scorners have pressed
From the wrongs of the helpless, the rending
And sobs of the fatherless breast.

We heap our table before you.
Eat and be filled: we go.

O friend, that had pity on us,
It is we that have pity on you!

Host [Alone, after a long silence, raising his head]
O what furious serpent's nest
Have I found in my own breast?
Like flames my thoughts upon me leap.
To eat my joy, to kill my sleep.
How dreadful is the silence here!
It weighs like terror on my ear.
Soon will the dawn be shining in.
And men awake, and birds begin;
And I must face the world afresh.
I faint, I fear it in my flesh.
I thought that I could love my kind!
Love is vast, and I was blind.
O mighty world, my weakness spare!
This love is more than I can dare.

VARIOUS POEMS

THE RENEWAL

No more of sorrow, the world's old distress,
Nor war of thronging spirits numberless,
Immortal ardours in brief days confined,
No more the languid fever of mankind
To-day I sing: 'tis no melodious pain
Cries in me: a full note, a rapturous strain
My voice adventures. Tremblest thou, my heart,
Because so eagerly the bliss would start
Up from thy fountains? O be near to me,
Thou that upliftest, thou that sett'st me free!

Out of the dim vault and the dying hues
Of Autumn, that for every wanderer strews
On silent paths the perishing pale leaves,
Fallen, like thoughts the heart no more believes,
From blackened branches to the frozen ground:
Out of the multitudinous dim sound
Of millions, to each other all unknown,
Warring together on the alien stone
Of streets unnumbered; where with drooping head
Prisoners pass, by unseen tyrants led
And with inaudible manacles oppressed.
Where he who listens cannot ever rest

For hearing in his heart the cry of men,
His brothers, from their lamentable den;
Out of all these I come to this sweet waste
Of woods and waters, and the odour taste
Of pines in sunshine hearkening to the roar
Of ocean on his solitary shore;
Lone beaches, where the yellow poppy blows
Unplucked, and where the wind for ever flows
Over the heathy desert; where the sea
Sparkles afar into infinity;
And the cleared spirit, tasting all things clean,
Rejoices, as if grief had never been;
Where thou, to whom the birds and the waves sing.
By some enchantment hast restored the Spring.

As when a dear hand touches on the hair
And thrills away the heaviness of care,
Till the world changes and through a window bright
The upleaping spirit gazes in delight.
Over my brain I feel a calming hand;
I look upon sweet earth and understand:
I hear the loud wind laughing through the trees;
The nimble air my limbs encourages.
And I upraise my songs afresh begun,
A palinode to the triumphant sun.

But thou, from whom into my soul to-day
Enters a quivering glory, ray on ray,
O by thine eyes a sister of the Spring,
Striking a core of sweetness in each thing
Thou look'st on, till it blossoms! By thy voice,
Soul of all souls created to rejoice!
Thou that with native over-brimming sense
Takest the light of Beauty's effluence.
As from the morning, in May's festal prime,
The young green leaves of the swift-budded lime;
That drawest all glad things, they know not why,
By some dear magnet of felicity;
And mournful spirits from their yoke of pain
Enchantest, till they lift their necks again.
And looking in thy bright and gentle eyes
To thee devote their dearest enterprise;
Thou whose brave heart could its own pain consume
And turn to deeper tenderness; in whom
Looks, thoughts, and motions, speech and mien persuade.
Immortal Joy hath his own mansion made:
How shall my too full heart, my stammering tongue.
Render thee half the song which thou hast sung

Into my being, by no web of words
Hindered, and fluid as the note of birds?
Or tell what magic of sweet air is shed
On me, so radiantly comforted?
I need each beam of the young sun; I need
Each draught of the pure wind, whereon to feed
My joy; each sparkle of the dew that shines
Under your branches, dark, sun-drunken pines.
All voices, motions of the unwearied sea;
But most, O tender spirit, I need thee.
For thou to this dumb beauty art the tone
It fain would render; all that is thine own

Of wayward and most human and most sweet
Mingling, until the music be complete:
Thine accents, O adorable and dear.
Command me to rejoice and have no fear;
Out of remembrance wash the soil of pain
And medicine me to my own self again.
Muse of my quickened verse, I am as he
Who, striving in the vast up-swollen sea,
Lifted a moment on a wave, descries
Unrolling suddenly the boundless skies.
Now is mere breathing joy; and all that strife
Confused and darkling, that we miscall life,
Is as a cloak, cast off in the warm spring.
Thus to possess the sunlight, is a thing
Worth more than our ambitions; more than ease
Wrung from the despot labour, the stale lees
Of youthful bliss: more than the plotting mind
Can ever compass, or the heart can find
In wisest books or multitude of friends.
For this it is that brings us to the lap
Of bounteous Earth, and fills us with her sap
And early laughter; melts the petty ends
Of daily striving into boundless air,
Revealing to the soul what it can dare:
Frees and enriches thousandfold; and steeps
This trembling self in universal deeps;
Lends it the patience of the eternal hills
To bear, no more in solitude, its ills,
And with all fervours of the world inspires
Its re-awakened and divine desires.
This is it that can find the deepest root
In us, and urge unto the fairest fruit,
Persuading the shut soul, that hid in night,
To crowd its blissful leaves into the light,
And shed, upon the lost, immortal seeds:

Kindles into a forge of fiery deeds
The smouldering heart, and closes the long wound
Of gentle spirits by rough time untuned;
And, O more precious even yet than this.
Empowers our weakness to support in bliss
The immensity of love, to love in vain
Yet still to hunger for that priceless pain;
To love without a bound, to set no end
To our long love, never aside to bend
In loving, but pour forth in living streams
Our hearts, as the full morn his quenchless beams.

He that this light hath tasted, asks no more
Dim questions answerless, that have so sore
Perplexed our thinking: in his bosom flow
Springs of all knowledge he hath need to know.
Nor vaunts he the secure philosophy
Self-throned, that would so easily untie
The knot of this hard world: and judging straight
Pronounce its essence and declare its fate.
How should the universal heart be known
To him that can so hardly read his own?
For where is he that can the inmost speak
Of his own being? Words are blind and weak,
Perplexing phantoms, dim as smoke to fire,
Mocking our tears, and torturing our desire,
When soul with soul would mingle: even Love
Never availed yet, howsoe'er he strove.
But, like the moon, to yield one radiant part
To the dark longing of the embracing heart.
And Earth, shall her vast secret open lie
Before the brief gaze of mortality?
Yet wayward and self-wise, no sooner stept
Into the world, and a few troubles wept,
A few unripe joys garnered, a few sins
Experienced, the impetuous mind begins
Its hasty wisdom; the world's griefs and joys
Holds in a balance, and essays to poise.
O persevering folly! never sleep
Must weigh the lids of that soul who would reap
This mystery; deserts vast must she explore.
Many far towns, many an unguessed shore.
And those deep regions search, more desolate far.
Where lives are herded, ignorant what they are,
And scarcely disentangling joy from woe;
Their being must she put on, if she would know
Humanity; most private bliss invade,
And with extremest terror be afraid.

Blank quiet and fierce rages apprehend.
Nor less into the leaping air ascend
Of flame-like spirits, and enamoured veins
Feel pulse in her; to exquisitest pains
Surrender. Then must her fleet impulse find
A way into the solitary mind
Of creatures, that in thousand thousand forms
Dumb life inspires and a brief sunshine warms;
And into the blind springs of sap and seed
Empty her passion, helpless with their need,
Torn with their hunger, thirsting with their thirst;
And deeper, whither eye hath never pierced.
Search out, amid the unsleeping stir that fills
Caves of old ocean and the rooted hills,
Whether indeed these streams of being flow
From inmost joy or a great core of woe.
Not until then is her wide errand sped,
Nor even so the supreme verdidt said.
For far into the outer night must fare
The uncompleted spirit, that to dare
Has but begun: now her commissioned bark
She must adventure on an ocean dark,
Illumined only by the driving foam
Of stars imprisoned in the invisible home
Each of his circle; age be lost in age
Ere she accomplish half her pilgrimage;
Nor till the last of those uncounted spheres
Its incommunicable joys and tears
Yield up to her, shall she at length return
And homeward heavy with the message burn,
And to her wonder-waiting peers rehearse
The mighty meaning of the Universe.

O lovely Joy! and sweet Necessity,
That wakes, empowers, and impassions me,
It is enough that this illumined hour
I feel my own life open like a flower
Within me. Whether the worlds ache or no,
Wearing a bright mask over breasts of woe,
I have no need to learn; I only gaze
Into thine eyes, dear spirit, that dost upraise
My spirit; thy bright eyes, that never cease
To thrill me with soft moonlike beams of peace.
I look in them as into Earth's own eyes;
Faith instantly my longing fortifies;
And now I think no single day has hours,
Nor year has days, nor life has years, for powers
Of joy sufficing; for the things begun

And waiting to be seen and felt and done.
O give me all thy pains, let them be mine.
And keep alone beloved delight for thine!
I have a flame within me shall transmute
All to an ash, that shall bear flower and fruit,
While thou look'st on me, while from thee there flows
The invisible strength that in my spirit grows,
Until like Spring, the blissful prodigal,
It burns as it were capable of all
That ever could be reached, enjoyed, or won.
Or known, or suffered, underneath the sun.

But O why tarry we in language vain
And speak thus dimly of delight and pain?
Those human words have fallen out of sense.
Drunk up into intenser elements.
As colours perish into perfect light.
Now in the visitation of swift sight
That makes me for this happy moment wise
Beyond all wisdom of philosophies,
I feel even through this transitory flesh
The pang of my creation dart afresh;
The bonds of thought fall off, and I am free;
There is no longer grief nor joy for me,
But one infinity of life that flows
From the deep ocean-heart that no man knows
Out into these unnumbered semblances
Of earth and air, mountains and beasts and trees,
One timeless flood which drives the circling star
In furthest heaven, and whose weak waves we are,
Mortal and broken oft in sobbing foam.
Yet ever children of that central home,
Our Peace, that even as we flee, we find;
The Road that is before us and behind.
By which we travel from ourselves, in sleep
Or waking, toward a self more vast and deep.

O could my voice but sound to all the earth
And bring thy tidings, radiant One, to birth
In hearts of men! How would they cast away
The shroud that wraps them from the spacious day.
Burst the strong meshes they themselves have spun
Of idle cares, and step into the sun.
And see, and feel, and dedicate no more
Their travail to some far imagined shore,
Some dreamed-of goal beyond life's eager sphere.
For lo! at every hour the goal is here;
And as the dark woods tremble to the morn,

That shoots into their dewy depths forlorn
Along the wind's path bright vi6torious rays,
And in all branches the birds lift their praise,
So should they sing, rejoicing to be free.
As I, beloved Muse, rejoice in thee.

FEBRUARY MORNING

Peacefully fresh, O February morn,
Thy winds come to me: quiet the light slants
Through silver-bosomed clouds, that slowly borne
Across the wide heath, endlessly advance.

Now 'tis that pause before the leaping Spring,
When over all things waiting comes a hush;
And shyly, listen! the one vocal thing,
Over his dewy notes lingers the thrush.

Now life, with all her hindering riddles, seems
Simple as its green budding to the tree.
Awhile the Fates forbear, and to my dreams,
Sheltered awhile from truth, relinquish me.

In haven and at anchor rides my heart,
And broods upon its swelling joys apart.

SONG

Love, like cordial wine,
Pouring his soul in mine,
Bids me to sing;
Youth's bright glory snatch,
And Time's paces match
With fearless wing.

Now, while breath is bliss.
And dawn wakes me with a kiss,
Ere this rapture flee.
Ere my heart thou claim.
Sorrow, I will aim
A shaft at thee.

MAY EVENING

So late the rustling shower was heard;
Yet now the aery west is still.
The wet leaves flash, and lightly stirred
Great drops out of the lilac spill.
Peacefully blown, the ashen clouds
Uncurtain height on height of sky.
Here, as I wander, beauty crowds
In freshness keen upon my eye.

Now the shorn turf a glowing green
Takes in the massy cedar shade;
And through the poplar's trembling screen
Fires of the evening blush and fade.
Each way my marvelling senses feel
Swift odour, light, and luminous hue
Of leaf and flower upon them steal:
The songs of birds pierce my heart through.

The tulip clear, like yellow flame,
Burns upward from the gloomy mould:
As though for passion forth they came,
Red hearts of peonies unfold:
And perfumes tender, sweet, intense
Enter me, delicate as a blade.
The lilac odour wounds my sense,
Of the rich rose I am afraid.

LOVE INFINITE

Where the honeysuckle blows
In the summer night, entwined
With fresh leaves of the rose,
Greenness in gloom divined;
Sweet breaths in a mystery conspire
My soul to ravish in swift desire

Yet I, as the hidden grass
I roam, within me bear
Joys that all these surpass.
And taste diviner air.
I love, I am loved: ah, nothing was ever sweet
As the word my lips to my heart repeat.

To take into my arms
The body of my bliss;
Charm beyond earthly charms,
Thought beyond thought were this.
My bliss not Earth in her ring could hold,
Nor Night, that doth all the stars enfold.

It clothes me and bathes me round:
I find no end nor measure.
I sink, I am lost; drowned
In the wonder and depth of pleasure.
O joy of love, could I plumb with a rod the sea.
My tongue might tell the untellable sweetness of thee.

OVER THE SEA

There came an evening when the storm had died
After long rain, miraculously clear:
And lo, across the burning waters wide
Rose up that coast, to thee and me how dear.

I knew the very houses by the bay.
And as I gazed, the time that clouded thick
On those old hours, fell suddenly away,
And memory was bared, even to the quick.

There was no peace then in the evening light;
For all my joy was left on that far shore.
Betwixt that apparition and the night
Alone I was; and I was brave no more.

Could I not keep thee, even in my heart?
O, my dear love, we perish, when we part.

LAMENT

O could the fallen leaf
On the bough again be born,
The old joy, the old grief
Come fresh to the heart with morn!
Spring will bring new flowers
And morning a new song:
But I want not these, I long

For the old days, the old hours.

The kisses that I kissed,
The sweet kisses you gave.
All are gone in a mist,
Gone into Time their grave.
Could I once again
Feel that old first kiss,
This, and only this
Could heal my wound of pain.

SEPARATION

We parted at golden dawn.
I feasted my last on her eyes,
And journeyed, journeyed alone:
Mountains and cities and skies

Hurried with cruel pace,
Endless and swift as the years,
From the light, from the sun, from her face,
My heart full of darkness and tears.
In a day, in a night have flown
Ages on ages fleet.
At dawn I wander alone
In a strange, in a silent street.

O love, far off in the clime
Of our joy, remember, and bend
From that early glory of Time
To me at his desolate end.

FEARS OF LOVE

Love grasps my heart in a net
Like the strong roots of a flower;
So surely his root is set
In my spirit, to hold me with power.
Yet to-night, O forgive me, Dear!
I am troubled, my heart trembles.
There flutters within me a fear
That Love in vain dissembles.

O is it that even our trust,

So strongly planted.
How steadfast soever, must
By its own fear be haunted?
As the heart must beat in the breast
If the pulse to its life be true.
Love must tremble and throb in his nest
To be sure of his life-blood anew?

IN THE FIRELIGHT

So sad and so lonely, Dear?
What dream by the fire do you dream
So deep, that you could not hear
My step as I entered? Dim
Is the room and the ceiling above you
With shadows that leap from the fire:
But hither, look hither, 'tis I
That am here; it is I, that love you.
I am come on the wings of desire:
Far off, I felt you sigh.

How could my heart refuse
Your longing that pierced so far?
That in those clear eyes, that muse,
Has kindled a mournful star?
But now, O now no longer
In the fire your comfort seek.
I bring love brighter than flame,
Than the sunshine warmer and stronger.
I cherish your hands; O speak,
Look on me, and speak my name!

THE ELM

O that I had a tongue, that could express
Half of that peace thou ownest, darkling Tree!
A slumber, shaded with the heaviness
That droops thy leaves, hangs deeply over me.

Far off, the evening light
Takes dim farewell: with hesitating Night
Day softly parleys; each her hour suspends,
Hushing the harboured winds, lest they affright

Ripe summer, that the falling leaf attends.

Fresh are the fields; and like a bloom they wear
This delicate evening. Peace upon them lies
So soft, I marvel that their slopes to air
Dissolve not, ere foot reach them: dewy skies

In dream the distance steep.
Thou only, solitary Elm, dost keep
Firm root in earth, and with thy musing crest
Unmoved, and darkly branching arms asleep,
As truth in dream, my spirit anchorest.

O surely Sleep inhabits in thy boughs.
Sleep, that knows all things; each well-hid distress
And private sigh; that all men's plea allows,
And is acquainted with the happiness
Removed, of him that grieves.

Surely beneath thy grave and tranquil leaves
He will unfold the obstinate mystery
That to our questing thought for ever cleaves,
And I may hold in my own hand the key.

To pierce the veil, and, seeing with clear eyes,
Wonder that riddles ever vext our lot,
What joy! For did perfidious Earth devise
Our desolation; were her felon plot

To flatter with fair shows.
That we her purpose out of useless woes
Might fashion, baited by a glorious lure,
You could not, O dark leaves, such deep repose
Imitate, nor conspire to seem secure.

You, as a child exclaims the natural fear
Which men dissemble, what you could not hide
Would utter: but you sleep, remote from care.
Still tree, by thy dumb augury I abide

Nor further ask thee tell
Things for the time imprisoned: I the spell
Might break, and thou the rash intruder scorn.
Enough, that what I know not thou know'st well,
Unagitated, nor hast need to mourn.

Mother, because thine eyes are sealed in sleep,
And thy cheeks pale, and thy lips cold, and deep
In silence plunged, so fathomlessly still
Thou liest, and relaxest all thy will,
Is it indeed thy spirit that is flown?
And gazing on thy face, am I alone?
O wake and tell me it is false: I fear;
And yet my heart persuades me thou art near
With living love. I cannot weep nor wail.
Nor feel thee taken from me; the tears fail
Within me, and my lips their moan reject.
Nay, as I watch, each instant I expert
Thine eyes will shine upon me unaware
And thy lips softly part, and to thy hair
Laying one hand, like those who come from dreams
So bright, that the dim morning only seems.
Thou wilt stretch forth the other into mine.
And to thy tender gaze thy love resign.
And speak, as thou wast wont, in thy low voice
Words wise and gentle, and my heart rejoice
With comfort poured into a trusted ear.
Mother, thou hearest? Surely thou dost hear.
Though thy tired eyes, blissfully closed, defer
The heavy world, the weight of human lot.
A change has fallen, and yet I know not what.
The deep communion of thy calm enfolds
My spirit also, and suspended holds
Lament, that knows not why to weep, yet yearns
For something missed, a fear it dimly learns.

And yet time has not touched us: the full glow
Salutes us, even as when five eves ago.
By this same window, over the same seas.
With thoughts of home brought by the shadowy breeze
From regions dearer than these golden skies.
We looked, and the same glory filled our eyes.
Even so the sun transfiguring the land
Upon the outstretched waters and bright sand
Reclined: the same faint odours floated sweet
From the green garden flowering at our feet.
Silent we gazed, and the serene large air
Appeased our thoughts; the burden that they bare
Departed: marvelling at our own release
We greeted wave and ray as kindred. Peace
Descended then, and touched us; and we knew
Our joy, attired in light, and felt it true.

Dust of the journey, the hot din of Rome
Fell from us: with an aspe6l kind, like home.
The silent and interminable sea
Our longing matched with his immensity:
We followed the far sails that, one by one.
Were drawn into the huge and burning sun;
And our souls set to freedom; and they cast
Away the soiled remembrance of things past,
And to the things before, with radiant speed,
Ran on in joy, eager as captives freed.
Far to the last horizon's utmost bound.
Onward and onward, and no limit found

Then thou rememberest how regarding ong
This lovely earth, an inward vision strong
O'ercame us, till terrestrial beauty took
An insubstantial seeming, the far look
Of regions known in dream. Forsaking fear
We rose together to that ampler sphere.
Where the sun burns, and in his train the moon
And myriad stars upon the darkness strewn
Illumine earth: on splendour past access
Of fleshly eye, revolving weariless,
We gazed; yet even as we gazed, the pang
Of the eternal touched us: then we sprang
From those bright circles, and each boundary passed
Of sense, and into liberty at last,
To our own souls we came, the haunted place
Of thought, companionless as ancient space.
Her lonely mirror; and uplifted thence
Sighed upward to the eternal Effluence
Of life, the intense glory that imbues
With far-off sheddings of its radiant hues
Mortality; that from the trees calls forth
Young leaves, and flowers from the untended earth;
And from the heart of man, joy and despair.
Rapture and adoration, the dim prayer
Of troubled lips, tears and ecstatic throes,
And fearful love unfolding like the rose.
And hymns of peace: whose everlasting power
Draws up ten thousand spirits every hour,
As the bright vapour from ten thousand streams,
Back to their home of homes, where thou with beams
Of living joy, O Sun of humankind,
Feedest the fainting and world-wounded mind,
And from remembrance burnest out all fear.
Sustained a moment in that self-same sphere
By wings of ecstasy, we hung, we drew

Into our trembling souls the very hue
Of Paradise, permitted the dear breath
Of truth; us also ignorance of death
Made mighty, and joy beyond the need of peace.
We of the certain light of blessedness
A moment tasted: then, since even desire
Perishes of its own exceeding fire.
Sighing our spirits failed, and fell away,
And sank into the tinge of alien day
Unwillingly, to memory and the weight
Of hope on the unsure heart, to armed fate.
And prisoning time, and to the obscuring sound
Of human words, O even to the ground!

The flame that fledged to that remotest height
Our spirits winged upon impassioned flight,
Sped us no more; but yet the usurping press
Of mortal hours their wonted heaviness
Relaxed, and on our rapture lightly leaned.
Now, as we gazed, a glory intervened:
We saw, yet saw not: our thoughts lingered, where
The rays yet pierced them of celestial air;
And with hearts hushed, as children that have learned
The meaning of some fear or joy, we turned
To one another, and spoke softly, and drew
Sighs, when that light smote on our thoughts anew.

O could the tumult of the senses sleep.
We murmured then: the mutinous body keep
Due pace, and this surrounding bath of light.
And these unwearying waves of day and night,
Following in beauty, the bright death and birth
Of suns, the sweet apparel of the earth.
Awhile be dimmed: could but the moon forego
Her splendour, and the winds forget to blow,
Ocean no more his troubling water heave,
And air its many-coloured web unweave,
Could but those visions pale that with affright
Pierce us, or unapproachable delight,
And all disturbing charm that at our eyes
Darts arrows, and for ever laughs and flies;
Could all be hushed, and memory turn her face,
And hope her low flute silence for a space.
And the soul slip the clinging leash of thought,
And cast the raiment she herself hath wrought.
And, as a flower springs upward unaware,
Naked ascend into the eternal air:
While he, who all this lovely warp of earth

With pomp of time inweaves, and still from birth
Moves his creation to death's other door,
If he through perishable mouths no more
Should spealc: not dimly through the veil of sense
Reported, nor conjectured influence
Of stars, nor through the thunder, nor by dream,
Nor by whatever of prophetic theme
Angel or man melodiously hath sung.
But utter very words of his own tongue,
And hold communion with the mind he made.
As with the light such things as know not shade,
O were not this the joy of joy to win.
And Paradise indeed to enter in?

I too, I too, in my own feverish youth
That light desired; and fainted after truth.
Unripe in fervour: in a misty morn
Of passion and unrestful ferment borne
Hither and thither, many uncertain flames
Did I pursue, and stumbled among shames,
And wandered where my own rash spirit drove,
Misleading to sad joys. In love with Love,
I looked in many faces, searching him,
And passionately embraced with phantoms dim.
Nor knew what my heart hungered for. But thou,
Who understandest, who beginnest now
In glory visible to fill mine eyes.
Thou that obscure desire didst authorise.
And by degrees unto itself disclose.
O by that beam how momentary shows
The world: 'tis but the bush that burns with thee:
And I the sandals of mortality
Long to put off, and with these chains have done,
That bind me, and fly homeward to the sun.

Mother, but thou? O what a pang is this
That wounds me? Mother, of what cup of bliss
Hast thou partaken, that I may not taste?
could I penetrate thy peace, and haste
Thither where thou art gone! O now in vair
My heart swells with unconquerable pain.
My desolation now too well I know.
I cannot come where my soul chafes to go.
But lay my wet cheek down to thine, and feel
Thy cold cheek desolate my heart, and stea
Peace and delight away. Dost thou not move,
Thou that wert used to weep sad tears of love
For me that grieved thee? Now thou weep'st no more.

But I with all the hurt I caused thee sore,
Weep all thy tears afresh. The door is closed
Upon me fast, and darkness interposed!
Now terrible thy calm seems, and this peace
Of night dismays me, longing for release
That will not visit me. On earth and skies
The hush of slumber falls, on thy closed eyes.
My mother, on the shore and on the sea;
All things the night appeases, but not me.

THE PINE WOODS OF GRIJO

Our voices break on a stillness bright and strange
Of early morning. Pines upon either hand
People the sunshine: deep as eye can range,
Their lofty throngs in a darkling order stand.

Our sandy path, new-washed with rains of night,
Already is dry: but dewily shine its banks.
And cool, the shadows asleep upon stems upright,
Unevenly dapple the silent, endless ranks.

The shadows, they lie so lightly, I think if a wind
Blew hither, his breath would lift them, as all sad cares
Are lifted, blown from the cleared and eager mind,
That now unbidden its native pleasure dares.

O pines of ardent branches, that plume with green
The delicate blue of morning, and softly house
The warm light poured from a splendour half unseen;
forest still and scented, hear my vows!

My body is warm to my heart, and I rejoice.
I clothe myself with the light, as ye are clad:
As ye breathe forth your perfume, I my voice
Will utter in morning freshness, alert and glad.

As the thistledown melts in the air, of very lightness,
Is scattered the web that trouble has vainly spun;
And my spirit arising bold, and bathed in brightness,
Hymns the excellent, sweet, victorious sun.

CARVALHOS

Earth, I love thee well;
And well dost thou requite me.
I have no tongue to tell
How this day thou hast thrilled
With wonder, to delight me.
My heart, intensely stilled.

On the white-walled knoll I stand
And feel beneath me glowing
The noon-hushed, lovely land:
Hills beyond hills, and few
Far towns a faint crest showing
Faint in the rounding blue.

Blue sea and radiant sky.
Blue sky and mountain marry;
And the mind, raised up on high.
Onward and onward springs;
Where'er she choose to tarry,
On every side are wings.

To the sun the sun-bathed pines
Their strength and sweetness render.
From where the far foam shines
Like the rim of a dazzling shield,
All fervent things and tender
Life, joy, and perfume yield.

Me, too, with mastering charm
From husks of dead days freeing.
The sun draws up, to be warm
And to bloom in this sweet hour;
The stem of all my being
Waited to bear this flower.

Upward, a burning flame,
My spirit springs enkindled.
No more of place, nor name,
Nor time aware, it flees
Aloft, in the noon to be mingled.
In fire its fire to appease.

DOURO

The dripping of the boughs in silence heard
Softly; the low note of some lingering bird

Amid the weeping vapour; the chill fall
Of solitary evening upon all
That stirs and hopes and apprehends and grieves,
With pining odours of the ruined leaves
Have like a dew distilled upon my heart
The air of death: but now recoiling start
Longing and keen remembrance out of sighs;
And forward the desiring spirit flies
Toward the wild peace of that illumined shore,
Which, left behind her, yet still shines before;
To Douro, rushing through the mighty hills.
Now his great stream with fancied splendour fills
Even this brooding twilight; a swift ghost,
Journeying forever to the glimmering coast,
Where his majestic voice is heard afar,
Exulting dim upon that ocean bar.
O Douro, gliding by dark woods, and fleet
Beneath thy shadowy rocks in the noon heat.
How my heart faints to follow after thee
On one true course to my deep destined sea!
To take no care of dimness or sunshine,
Urged ever by an inward way divine,
Nor falter in this heavy gloom that brings
So thick upon me lamentable things
Of earth, and hinders the swift spirit's wings,
And clouds the steadfast vision that sustains
Alone the trembling heart amid perpetual pains.

Dear friend, who thirstest, even as I, to be
Heir and possessor of sweet liberty,
Once more in memory let us pluck the hour
That bloomed so perfect, and renew the power
Of joy within our wondering breasts, to feel
That freshness of eternal things, and heal
All our unhappy thoughts in those pure rays.
Not yet the last of these delightful days
Into the dark unwillingly has flown,
And thou and I upon a hill o'ergrown.
That indolently shadows Douro stream.
Together watch the wonderful clear dream
Of evening. Under the dark shore of pines
Noiselessly running, the wide water shines.
Curving afar, from where the mountains lift
Their burning heads, through many a forest rift
The River comes, scenting the spaces free
In this broad channel, of his welcoming sea.
No more by silent precipices hewn
Out of the night, murmuring a lonely tune

To craggy Fregeneda; nor where shines
Regoa, throned among her purple vines,
Impetuously seeking valleys new;
But smoothing his broad mirror to the hue
And peace of heaven, unhasting now he flows
And with the sky unfathomably glows,
Even as on yonder shore the woods receive
In their empurpled bosoms the warm eve.
As when a lover gazes tenderly
Upon his loved one, and, as tender, she
Hushes her heart, her joy to realize.
So hushed, so lovely, so contented lies
Earth, by that earnest-gazing glory blest.
But on this hither bank that fervent West
Is hidden behind us, and the stems around
Spring shadowy from the bare and darkling ground.
Only a single pine out of the shade
Emerges, in what splendour soft arrayed!
Magical clearness, warming to the sight
As to the touch it would be: plumed with light,
Motionless upward the tree soars and burns.
But now the dews upon the freshened ferns
In the dim hollow gather, and cool scent
Of herbage with the pine's pure odour blent
And voices of the villagers below
As home, with music, up the stream they row,
Greet us descending; every blossom sleeps,
And bluer and more blue the evening steeps
Water and fragrant grass and the straight stems
In tender mystery. Down a path that hems
The hollow, to our waiting boat we come.
Pale purple flames shining amid the gloom
Signal the autumn crocus: look, afar.
Betwixt the tree-tops, the first-ventured star!
Soon gliding homeward under shadowy shores
And deepened sky, to the repeated oars'
Strong chime we hasten. Now along pale sand
Our ripple leaps in silver; now the land.
High over the swift water darkly massed.
Echoes our falling blades as we go past;
Until, enthroned upon her hills divine.
The city nears us: lights begin to shine
Scarce from the stars distinguished, so the gloom
Has mingled earth and sky; more steeply loom
The banks on either side, at intervals
Tufted with trees, or crowned with winding walls;
And now at last the river opens large.
Filled with the city's murmur; from his marge,

Slope over slope, the glimmering terraces
Rise, and their scattered lamps' bright images
Cast on the wavering water; and we hear
The sound of soft bells, and cries faint or near
From the dim wharves, or anchored ships, whose spars
Entangle in dark meshes the white stars.
And pale smoke rising blue on the blue air
Sleeps in a thin cloud under heights that bear
Towers and roofs lofty against the west.
Where yet a clearness lingers. Now the breast
Of Douro heaves, foreboding whither bound
His currents hasten, and with joyous sound,
As though the encountering brine new pulses gave.
Lifts, to outrace our speed, his buoyant wave.
For, hearken, up the peaceful evening borne
Out of the wide sea-gates, low thunders warn
Of Ocean beating with his sleepless surge
Along the wild sand-marges: the deep dirge
Of mariners, that wakes the widow's ear
At night, far inland, terrible and near.
Fainter, this eve, he murmurs than as oft
His troubled music: here, by distance soft.
The abrupt volley, the sharp shattering roar.
And seethe of foam flung tumbling up the shore.
Mingle in one wide rumour, that all round
Is heard afar, robing the air with sound.
Deep in my heart I hear it. The still night
Deepens, as we ascend the homeward height.
And loud or low, in following intervals.
Over the hills the sound unwearied falls;
And as upon my bed my heavy eyes
Close up, the drowsing mind re-occupies.

O what a vision floats into my sleep!
As a night-shutting flower, my senses keep
The live day's lingering odours and warm hues.
That thought and motion with themselves transfuse.
Till sound and light and perfume are but one.
Mingled in fires of the embracing sun.
Yet still I am aware of Ocean stirred
Far off, and like a grave rejoicing heard.
Am I awake, or in consenting dreams
Pour thither all my thought's tumultuous streams?
His voice, to meet them, a deep answer sends:
My soul, to listen, her light wing suspends.
And, pillowed upon undulating sound.
For all desire hath satisfaction found.
He calls her thither, where the winds uncage

Vast longing, that the unsounded seas assuage.
Breeze after breeze her winged pinnace bears
Over the living water, that prepares
Still widening mystery: she her speed the more
Urges, exulting to have lost the shore.
Supported by the joy that sets her free,
Delighted mistress of her destiny.
Fills the wide night with beating of her wing,
And is content, for ever voyaging
By timeless courses, over worlds unknown.
Lifted and lost, abounding and alone.

NATURE

Because out of corruption burns the rose,
And to corruption lovely cheeks descend;
Because with her right hand she heals the woes
Her left hand wrought, loth nor to wound nor mend;

I praise indifferent Nature, affable
To all philosophies, of each unknown;
Though in my listening ear she leans to tell
Some private word, as if for me alone.

Still, like an artist, she her meaning hides.
Silent, while thousand tongues proclaim it clear;
Ungrudging, her large feast for all provides;
Tender, exultant, savage, blithe, austere,

In each man's hand she sets its proper tool,
For the wise, wisdom, folly for the fool.

Laurence Binyon – A Short Biography

Robert Laurence Binyon, CH, was born on August 10th, 1869 in Lancaster in Lancashire, England to Quaker parents, Frederick Binyon and Mary Dockray.

He studied at St Paul's School, London before enrolling at Trinity College, Oxford, to read classics.

Binyon's first published work was Persephone in 1890. Whilst only a few pages in length it certainly illustrated the talents that Binyon would develop as a poet even though he continued to advance multiple career opportunities.

Immediately after graduating in 1893, Binyon started work at the British Museum for the Department of Printed Books, writing catalogues for the museum and art monographs for himself. As well as being one of England's best poets he was also renowned for his knowledge of various arts particularly with regard to Japan and Persia.

His first poetry book Lyric Poems was published in 1894.

In 1895 his first art book, Dutch Etchers of the Seventeenth Century, was published and, that same year, Binyon moved into the Museum's Department of Prints and Drawings.

Whilst Binyon became known to a wide audience as a poet his output was not prodigious. In 1898, Porphyrion & Other Poems was published followed by Odes (1901) and The Death of Adam & Other Poems (1904).

That same year, 1904, Binyon married the historian Cicely Margaret Powell. The union was to produce three daughters.

In the early years of the 20th Century Binyon was a regular patron of the Wiener Cafe of London together with fellow artists and intellectuals; Ezra Pound, Sir William Rothenstein, Walter Sickert, Charles Ricketts, Lucien Pissarro and Edmund Dulac.

His poetic work continued despite the demands of the British Museum and his other interests. London Visions was published in 1908 followed by England & Other Poems in 1909.

His work at the British Museum ensured promotions were a frequent occurrence for Binyon. In 1909, he became its Assistant Keeper, and in 1913 he was made the Keeper of the new Sub-Department of Oriental Prints and Drawings.

It was also at this time that he played a crucial role in the formation of Modernism in London by introducing young Imagist poets such as Ezra Pound, Richard Aldington and H.D. (Hilda Doolittle) to East Asian visual art and literature.

Many of Binyon's books produced while at the Museum were influenced by his own sensibilities as a poet, although some are clearly works of plain scholarship, such as his four volume catalogue of all the Museum's English drawings, and his seminal catalogue of Chinese and Japanese prints.

Binyon's poetic reputation before the war, although built on several slim volumes, was such that, on the death of the Poet Laureate Alfred Austin in 1913, Binyon was among the names considered as his likely successor. It was quite a field. Among the other illustrious contenders were Thomas Hardy, John Masefield and Rudyard Kipling; however the post was awarded to Robert Bridges.

Moved and shaken by the onset of the World War I and its military tactics of young men slaughtered to hold or gain a few yards of shell-shocked mud as the British Expeditionary Force began its campaign Binyon wrote his seminal poem For the Fallen, with its Ode of Remembrance (the third and fourth or simply the fourth stanza of the poem). The poem was published by The Times newspaper on September 21st, when public feeling was shaken by the recent Battle of Marne. It became an instant classic, turning moments of great loss into a National and human tribute.

Today, For the Fallen, is often recited at Remembrance Sunday services as well as being an integral part of Anzac Day services in Australia and New Zealand and of November 11th Remembrance Day services in Canada. The "Ode of Remembrance" is now acknowledged as a tribute to all casualties of war, irrespective of nation.

In 1915, despite being too old to enlist, Binyon volunteered at a British hospital for French soldiers, the Hôpital Temporaire d'Arc-en-Barrois, Haute-Marne, France, working for a short time as a hospital orderly.

He returned there in the summer of 1916 and took care of soldiers taken in from the Verdun battlefield. He wrote about his experiences in For Dauntless France (1918) and his poems, "Fetching the Wounded" and "The Distant Guns", were inspired by his hospital service.

After the war, he returned to the British Museum and wrote numerous books on art; especially on William Blake, Persian and Japanese art. His work on ancient Japanese and Chinese cultures offered inspiration that inspired many, among them the poets Ezra Pound and W. B. Yeats. His work on Blake and his followers kept alive the then nearly-forgotten memory of the work of Samuel Palmer. Binyon's spectrum of interests continued the traditional interest of British visionary Romanticism in the rich strangeness of Mediterranean and Oriental cultures.

In 1931, his two volume Collected Poems appeared and by 1932, Binyon was promoted to the post of Keeper of the Prints and Drawings Department. The following year, 1933, he retired from the British Museum. He went to live in the country at Westridge Green, near Streatley but continued writing poetry.

In 1933–1934, Binyon was appointed Norton Professor of Poetry at Harvard University. He delivered a series of lectures on The Spirit of Man in Asian Art, which were published in 1935.

Binyon continued his academic work: in May, 1939 he gave the prestigious Romanes Lecture in Oxford on Art and Freedom, and in 1940 he was appointed the Byron Professor of English Literature at the University of Athens. He worked there until forced to leave by the German invasion of Greece in April, 1941.

Binyon had been friends with Ezra Pound for a long time, and in the 1930s the two became especially close; Pound affectionately called him "BinBin", and he assisted Binyon with his translation of Dante.

Between 1933 and 1943, Binyon published his acclaimed translation of Dante's Divine Comedy in an English version of terza rima, made with some editorial assistance by Ezra Pound. It was acknowledged for many decades as *the* popular translation for Dante readers.

During the horrors of the Second World War Binyon wrote a poem that many claim as to be a masterpiece 'The Burning of the Leaves', puts in print his lines on the London Blitz.

At his death Binyon was working on a major three-part Arthurian trilogy, the first part of which was published after his death as The Madness of Merlin (1947).

Robert Laurence Binyon died in Dunedin Nursing Home, Bath Road, Reading, on March 10th, 1943 after undergoing an operation. A funeral service was held at Trinity College Chapel, Oxford, on March 13th, 1943.

Binyon's ashes were scattered at St. Mary's Church, Aldworth.

On November 11th, 1985, Binyon was among sixteen poets of the Great War commemorated on a slate stone unveiled in Westminster Abbey's Poets' Corner. The inscription on the stone quotes a fellow Great War poet, Wilfred Owen. It reads: "My subject is War, and the pity of War. The Poetry is in the pity."

Laurence Binyon – A Concise Bibliography

Poems and Verse
Persephone (1890)
Lyric Poems (1894)
The Praise of Life (1896)
Porphyrion & Other Poems (1898)
Odes (1901)
Death of Adam & Other Poems (1904)
Penthesilea (1905)
London Visions (1908)
England & Other Poems (1909)
Auguries (1913)
For The Fallen (The Times, September 21st, 1914)
The Winnowing Fan (1914)
The Anvil (1916)
The Cause (1917)
The New World: Poems (1918)
The Secret: Sixty Poems (1920)
The Idols (1928)
Collected Poems Vol I: London Visions, Narrative Poems, Translations (1931)
Collected Poems Vol II: Lyrical Poems (1931)
The North Star & Other Poems (1941)
The Burning of the Leaves & Other Poems (1944)
The Madness of Merlin (1947)

Poems Set to Music
In 1915 Cyril Rootham set "For the Fallen" for chorus and orchestra, first performed in 1919 by the Cambridge University Musical Society conducted by the composer.

Edward Elgar set to music "The Fourth of August", "To Women", and "For the Fallen", as The Spirit of England, Op. 80, for tenor or soprano solo, chorus and orchestra (1917).

English Arts and Myth

Dutch Etchers of the Seventeenth Century (1895), Binyon's first book on painting
John Crone and John Sell Cotman (1897)
William Blake: Being all his Woodcuts Photographically Reproduced in Facsimile (1902)
English Poetry in its relation to painting and the other arts (1918)
Drawings and Engravings of William Blake (1922)
Arthur: A Tragedy (1923)
The Followers of William Blake (1925)
The Engraved Designs of William Blake (1926)
Landscape in English Art and Poetry (1931)
English Watercolours (1933)
Gerard Hopkins and his influence (1939)
Art and freedom. (The Romanes lecture, delivered 25 May 1939). Oxford: The Clarendon press, (1939)

Japanese and Persian Arts
Painting in the Far East (1908)
Japanese Art (1909)
Flight of the Dragon (1911)
The Court Painters of the Grand Moguls (1921)
Japanese Colour Prints (1923)
The Poems of Nizami (1928) (Translation)
Persian Miniature Painting (1933)
The Spirit of Man in Asian Art (1936)
Autobiography[edit]
For Dauntless France (1918) (War memoir)

Biography
Botticelli (1913)
Akbar (1932)

Stage Plays
Brief Candles A verse-drama about the decision of Richard III to dispatch his two nephews
Paris and Œnone. A Tragedy in One Act (1905)
Godstow Nunnery: Play
Boadicea; A Play in eight Scenes
Attila: A Tragedy in Four Acts (1907)
Ayuli: A Play in three Acts and an Epilogue
Sophro the Wise: A Play for Children
(Most of the above were written for John Masefield's theatre).

www.ingramcontent.com/pod-product-compliance
Lightning Source LLC
Chambersburg PA
CBHW060139050426

42448CB00010B/2200